Single, Seventy, and Sexless in Seattle!

It Can *Still* Happen for You Online
A Dating Guide for Women 40 and Beyond

MARY HYATT DOERRER

Single, Seventy, and Sexless in Seattle!
It Can Still Happen for You Online
A Dating Guide for Women 40 and Beyond

Publisher: Another Book
Editorial: Chin-Sun Lee
Cover Design: Kevin Smith

Author Photo: Natalie Post www.postproductions.com

www.maryhyattdoerrer.com

Publisher's Cataloging-In-Publication Data
(Prepared by The Donohue Group, Inc.)
Names: Doerrer, Mary Hyatt, author.
Title: Single, Seventy, and Sexless in Seattle! : it can still happen for you online : a dating guide for women 40 and beyond / Mary Hyatt Doerrer.
Description: First edition. | [Sammamish, Washington] : Another Book, [2021]
Identifiers: ISBN 9781736685709 (print) | ISBN 9781736685716 (ebook) | ISBN 9781736685723 (Kindle)
Subjects: LCSH: Online dating. | Older women--Social life and customs. | Interpersonal relations. | Mate selection.

Classification: LCC HQ801.82 .D64 2021 (print) | LCC HQ801.82 (ebook) | DDC 306.730285--dc23

Coming Around Again from the Paramount Picture HEARTBURN
Words and Music by Carly Simon
Copyright (c) 1986 Sony/ATV Harmony and C'est Music
All Rights by Sony/ATV Music Publishing LLC, 424 Church Street, Suite 1200, Nashville, TN 37219 International Copyright Secured All Rights Reserved
Reprinted by Permission of Hal Leonard LLC

Print ISBN 978-1-73668-570-9
eBook ISBN 978-1-73668-571-6
Kindle 978-1-73668-572-3
Printed by: www.Bookbaby.com
Printed in the United States of America

www.MaryHyattDoerrer.com
www.singleseventysexlessinseattle.com

DEDICATION

This book is dedicated to Linda, a friend for more than sixty years, who listened patiently when she probably didn't want to, and to all the women out there who might have just enough courage to take the leap and persist until they find their true match.

AUTHOR'S NOTE

Before this book was published, the Covid-19 pandemic in our world occurred. What we are going through in this pandemic may continue for a while, but eventually we will return to "normal" or a "new normal." Wherever you find yourself, either at present in the pandemic or after, it is possible to find a significant other who brings love into your life. Online dating during the pandemic means that you'll have a better chance getting to know someone *before* you meet them. This is a good thing and not something that should make you overly cautious. Be inventive and creative! There are ways you can get to know prospective matches: ask questions, keep your video camera off for your first few emails/messages, discuss what you would like to do on a first in-person date. What you can learn about each other before you meet face–to-face is limitless. The only way to get to the other side is knowing it will happen and using your intelligence to get there.

Depending on your generation, when you first started dating, online platforms may not have existed, or been as accessible. Now they're prevalent and available to everyone. The goal is to find a site that you find comfortable using. This book will help you navigate the online dating world during the pandemic and post-pandemic. It will give you general insight as to how dating has changed in modern times, whether online dating is a new or not so new experience for you. It will also help you sidestep some of the situations you can and should avoid *if* you learn what you need to know before jumping in. So open that mindset. Believe in yourself and know that it will happen. By being proactive and reading books like this before you take the leap, you should enjoy the process...*and* find your significant other.

CONTENTS

Introduction

"Sure!" was my out-of-body reply to a question I was asked by a stranger I had just met online.

The next day, I found myself flying all over Puget Sound in a tiny plane (think tin can with wings) and landing in Port Townsend, about 100 miles northwest of Seattle, for a quick bite to eat. He was a pilot and had rented a plane not owning one apparently due to two previous wives. This was so "not me," but I was determined to change my fear into fearless and start saying yes to everything that came my way as I entered the online dating world.

This book is for women of any age who don't know much about online dating, but particularly for those like me approaching dating later in life—who are in their forties and up through their eighties! Even men of any age can learn something too. It's for those, in any stage of life, who understand and may have tried online dating, but have become frustrated and just need some encouragement to not give up. Yes, there are women who, through no fault of their own—believe this, women, no fault of *your* own—are alone because of divorce, being widowed (my case), simply never having the desire to be married or in a relationship, or recovering from a recent short or long-term relationship breakup.

Anyone who is serious about finding love can learn what it takes to navigate the sometimes-murky waters of online dating by being pro-active and knowing who is out there and available. You *can* and *will* want to avoid some of the situations that are anxiety-producing and lead you in the wrong direction. Because of what I experienced in my first-time adventure in online dating, I didn't want other women to go through the same heartbreak. I want you to have the most positive experiences you can.

By learning and believing, and most importantly, *believing in yourself*, you will skip the heartbreak. But this book was written not to simply teach or help women to avoid heartbreak. It is about learning the mindset of trusting we are worthy women who want to live the best life we can and believing it is probable and possible. When we, as women, experience and know this, we expand our reach to all those who are in pain and looking for answers.

I was raised in a small town in Indiana, and pretty much lived in a white, privileged bubble since that time. I have been on a spiritual journey for the last ten years and have learned who I am and more about the world, and what I believe is important in life. I was surprised to find out how the world has changed in the dating scene. I wish I knew what I know now before I started the game of online dating. This is why I wrote this book.

I am not the good-looking forty-something dating coach (usually male) who went on 200 dates, finally found the ideal soulmate on date 201, got married, and now has the perfect family with children. Dating coaches can be told by women about their journeys and what happens when they date men. The coaches can be very helpful and useful, but actual firsthand knowledge counts and some things can only be learned from actually having lived them. Still, don't discount what these dating coaches have to offer. They have experience and do want the best for women who are on a quest to find someone they love and who loves them. The practical advice they offer to women of all ages will help them learn about relationships in general. Their stories are fun to listen to and can be enlightening. One coach I've watched innumerable times is Mat Boggs. He is smart, funny, and gives excellent advice to women seeking love online.

Most dating coaches—not all—are men in their forties or younger. And *not always*, but *primarily*, they focus on giving advice to younger females, usually age fifty and under. When you are in your forties and older, online dating can be difficult but still doable. It is undeniable that women forty and older simply will not have as many available men to choose from, but quality men *do* exist and they are looking for the same identical things you are—companionship and love.

The response rate from older acceptable men you would even consider meeting is much, much lower than for those who are younger. Don't be surprised to search through numerous dating profiles before finding someone appropriate. But they will appear! It is true many, or perhaps most, men will prefer younger women, and many younger women don't mind dating older men who are established, sometimes retired, and have financial resources. *But* this doesn't mean if you are over forty or fifty your search will be futile. See point #4 in Chapter 1.

Online dating has lost its stigma and reputation of being a waste of time and too much trouble. For one thing, if you know you are worthy and are open to learning a few valuable insights, you can find men who are worth the search—right in your own home with your computer. Just don't give up. If you prefer to snack on bonbons on a couch, by yourself, watching your favorite reality shows, or binging on Netflix, *stop reading this immediately!* If you want to find your significant other, *then keep reading.* I have real experience and have learned maybe more than I have wanted to, but I can help you achieve your goal of finding a good partner. I turned seventy on January 1st and thought…it is time!

I'll start out by encouraging you to take steps to become comfortable in the world of online dating. Whether this is new to you or not, you will need support and encouragement when you face difficult times. After discovering ways to increase your courage, we'll move on to potential dating scenarios and other influencing factors including how the brain works and how we learn. Then we'll progress to the logistics of how to get started; looking for the dating site that fits you the best and is the easiest to use. Next, you'll learn about writing your profile, posting your outstanding photos, and making sure you give an idea of who you are and what traits you're looking for in whom you would like to meet. The dating site you choose will lead you through various questions, and it's up to you to come across as being committed, honest, and interested in the process. Once you have your profile completed, I'll lead you through various ways to communicate. The mantra of this book is: *believe* in yourself and *believe* it can happen for you!

I hope by the time you have completed this book, you will:

- Feel more comfortable navigating the online dating world.

- Understand how important it is that you come across as interesting and attractive in your profile and how to accomplish this.

- Accept that "wishing" it so will not make your match appear. You will learn why being proactive will get you where you want to be.

- Have confidence in using your intuition but also be aware of "red flags" you will come across.

- Learn to appreciate men you will meet and how you can actually enjoy the process by conquering your fears.

Back to my official first online date. It all started on a Friday night glancing through the profiles of the age sixty-seven and above "qualifying" men on a dating site. I felt that I had waited long enough, four years after my husband's death, and I was ready to meet someone. I hadn't been online long, maybe three months, but long enough to know that most men wanted to come across as looking cool or sophisticated, or athletic. This guy's photos were hilarious. Bending over backwards fixing a neighbor's stove, (he later told me he had accidentally started a fire in his attempt to fix it), before–and–after photos of his face-lift— Tom Cruise was the "after" photo—and then some regular photos of his family, etc. I quickly emailed him and told him how much he had made me laugh.

We emailed back and forth a few times that night and then he wrote, "I know this sounds crazy, but would you like to go flying tomorrow?" And that is when I said "Sure!" He said he would call me the next morning to let me know the details. After taking my grandson to his swimming lesson Saturday morning in Snoqualmie, a small town about thirty-five miles east of Seattle, we made arrangements to meet at the airfield. It certainly was one of the best days of the summer...beautiful blue skies and sunny, the reason why many of us live in Seattle. He was a gentleman in every way and I intuitively sensed he knew what he was doing while flying the tin can—I mean plane. (Update: We recently did a replay of our first date that occurred almost a year ago and had an even better time on the replay!)

Things happen in our lives that we are not ready to deal with or face, but as women, we learn to adjust and move forward. My husband died due to an illness when we were both sixty-five and I knew exactly zero widows, single men, or single women my age. The area where I live is occupied primarily by married couples, many with young families, or older retired long-time marrieds. Because I raised a family and didn't work outside the home, ninety-five percent of my friends were married. Many of my single good friends live out of state. It took such a long time to get through and past his death that all of a sudden, I was seventy and knew I did not want to live the rest of my life alone, even with my kids close by, my many good friends, my wonderful neighbors, and my involvement in the local community. Speaking of friends, let's talk about that.

When I told my friends in my coffee group (yes, they are all married) about the pilot—it was somewhat humorous to me that they were fascinated but horrified that I would do such a thing!

"Well, he is probably a psychopath. Okay, if not a psychopath, definitely a sociopath."

"He could have just opened the door and thrown you out and no one would have ever known what happened to you...basically shark bait!"

And then a friend, whose husband had been a commercial pilot for years, spoke up and said, "You did have a rather expensive first date because renting a plane would have cost a minimum of $600 for four hours."

I meekly replied, "I did offer to pay for lunch."

That first date was the beginning of a journey that would lead me to share my experiences with you here.

Chapter 1—The Beginning

1. Support When You Start Online Dating

If you are already online or thinking about online dating, know that most, if not all, of your married friends may not understand this. Even single friends might wonder what is wrong with you. Find someone who you are close to or even a counselor/therapist to get you through the rough spots. *And* if you're like many, you *will* have some hard times. I had a very good friend, albeit married, who was patient and at least tried to understand what I was going through, who listened and tried not to judge. My other good friends listened and were patient, but still, they couldn't grasp why women would even want to have anything to do with online dating, or at this stage in life, *men!* I also had a life coach for three months who knew something about online dating as she was divorced and had experienced it herself. And my longtime therapist, since my husband's death, was invaluable.

2. Be Proactive

Before testing the waters and sticking your toe in, read everything you can about online dating. Relationship books online and off can give you a start if it has been a while since you have dated. Listen to as many podcasts centered on online dating and relationships as you can. Besides learning the logistics of online dating, there are also many fun-to-read books about how men think and why they do what they do—written by men.

You will learn to evaluate men by their profiles, ones that you might find appealing and have enough in common with to at least meet for coffee at your local Starbucks or other hangout. You will run across many men that you know immediately are not for you and/or some you are not sure about at first, until you find what you are looking for—a stable, caring man who wants what you do. Read these books to get a basic understanding. I did not have a clue what I was doing...I made mistakes I could have avoided. Don't waste several months brokenhearted over someone who is not worth your efforts. You are in charge of your love life. When you learn the "game," as harsh as it may seem, and know more about how to search and date desirable men, you can make it happen.

3. When Learning Something New

Even if you feel fairly confident, is it wise to think we already know everything before we start? That would be similar to a non-swimmer looking at the water and jumping in, only to find that she sinks right to the bottom. As the Girl Scout motto says, "Be Prepared." Learn what you will be facing before jumping in so you can be aware of, and consequently avoid, the pitfalls that will occasionally arise. Only by practice and the willingness to get past these temporary roadblocks will you be able to sail through the process and enjoy it.

Practice is invaluable in this realm because the more experiences and dates you have, the easier and more enjoyable dating will become. You will learn if the traits you are looking for show up in the men you date. Anxiety and fear can arise, but don't let this consume you. I have a friend who met her husband online. He was about to give up when they had their first date. They are now married, immensely happy, and are raising their family together. He has many anxiety-ridden memories from his online dating experiences that he still cannot talk about. So don't forget, both sexes can suffer this anxiety and fear. The main point to remember is to keep trying and don't give up.

4. Dating for Older Women

Or should I say wiser women? To pretend that age is not a factor in the dating realm would be untruthful. It can be more difficult for older women, the primary reason being that in our culture—in most cultures—men get to choose younger women without an eyebrow raised. So, if older men prefer younger women and seek them out, it is statistically reasonable that fewer older men are available to date women their age. And there are many younger women who do not have a problem dating men who are old enough to be their fathers, if not older. But there are men who prefer women their own age because they simply have more in common with them and realize that women their age have life experiences and wisdom that some younger women do not possess.

Remember, there are good and decent quality men who are not seeking women ten, twenty years younger or women half their age. Sometimes that may have something to do with age denial. Many men simply don't want to face the fact they are aging and are either consciously or subconsciously looking for someone who can help them forget that fact. But don't use this as a reason why you will find it impossible to find someone because secure, mature men can handle the aging process and appreciate women who do the same.

If you are focused and proactive and dedicated to the process, you can and will find men who are attractive to you and who are attracted to you. It amazes me that women who profess they would like to be in a relationship make every excuse why they can't be in one: all the good men are taken, everyone is married, they can't be trusted, they won't like my kids, they are emotionally unavailable, etc. Yes, some of these are true, but don't waste your time believing in generalities. There are good men out there and if you are proactive, positive, open-hearted and believe in yourself—you will meet them. Just remember, don't ever give up even when you feel discouraged! Or rejected! Or think you're too old! Or too heavy! Or too whatever!

3

Below are some things you might want to consider before you decide to date online:

- Are you flexible? If not so much, do you at least realize this is a good attribute to have? Can you conceive of doing something new, something out of your comfort zone?

- Are you willing to be adaptable? That would include the willingness to meet someone you have never met before and someone who may not fit into your current mind-set about who is acceptable and who is not.

- Are you wounded from previous relationships with men? If so, are you trying to get past these traumas and seeking help?

- Are you at least somewhat up-to-date with the tech world, texting and computer use? If not, are you willing to seek help from those who have these skills and are able to help you?

- Are you able to accept your body? All the flaws and imperfections? The *average* dress size of an American woman is 12 to 14. Remember this. If your dress size is above or below these, does it matter?

- Are you excited about meeting new people, hearing their stories and appreciating them, and learning new things you have not known before?

- Are you willing to learn as much as you can about dating to increase your self-confidence before you try online dating?

- If you can answer these questions truthfully and honestly with a "yes," you are at least entering the "can do" stage and passing the "anxious, full of fear, no can do" stage.

5.   Online Dating: Worth Your Time and Effort?

It may take a change of attitude to understand this because many, including fellow singles, may question why you would even consider this approach to dating. It does work and statistics prove it. Just because your friends who have been married thirty or more years or wounded single friends think it's a terrible idea doesn't mean it is. Statistics suggest that one in five people found love on dating sites when trying online dating...why shouldn't you be one of them?

Fifty million Americans have tried online dating and its popularity rises every year. It also doesn't have the stigma that was once attached to it. Contrary to what your older married friends may think, forty-four percent of dating-age people have a positive attitude toward online dating. Stanford sociologist Michael Rosenfeld has found that heterosexual couples are more likely to meet a romantic partner online than through personal contacts and connections. Since 1940, traditional ways of meeting partners have all been in decline. Rosenfeld has researched dating and mating including the internet's effect on society for two decades.

6. Courage

One of my older friends recently said she doesn't like taking risks. Do we really not want to take risks for the remainder of our lives? How can we learn and grow without taking risks? And using our courage to face them? I love what Winston Churchill said about courage. It is the essential virtue because "it guarantees all the others." Without courage, how will we overcome and face our fears? How we will confront obstacles in our lives? How will we learn to do things we've never done before?

The online dating life, unless you are a seasoned veteran who knows all the ropes, does indeed take courage *and* the ability to take risks. It takes courage to face the rejection you will get...and give. And it takes courage to move forward from past relationships. The rejection, which goes both ways, can be very disheartening. Who wants to be rejected? Exactly *no one!* Believe it or not, it is hard to be rejected by someone you didn't even like. Not only do you not want to be rejected, it is difficult to reject those who may like you. Unless of course you have a cold heart which...well, we won't go there.

Without courage, you will be tempted to throw in the towel and say it's not worth it. But it is! *Love is worth it.* It is the human condition... we all want love. Some single men and women can be happy and thriving, many seem quite satisfied with their single status. They may have many good friends, family who live close by (or with them), and are involved in numerous activities. But if you are anyone like me, wanting companionship and love in all aspects of your life, then never give up your goal of finding it. It is up to you to figure out what you desire in your life and make it happen. I wanted a true, loving companion who I knew I could trust and travel with and who loved me unconditionally. It really gets down to what you want in your life. And realize, research reveals being alone and/or lonely can be a detriment to how long you will live.

7. Speaking of Never Giving Up

When you have made the decision to take the leap, remember, good things don't happen overnight. They might occasionally, but usually it takes patience and perseverance to get what you want. Isn't this a general rule of life? Stick to a plan, know what you want, and don't give up when things take longer than they should. Learning something new and different from what we have previously experienced usually takes time. Don't be one of those people who are "stuck." They insist on doing the same thing for years, whether it comes to dating or eating the same breakfast or anything else in their lives. Or they go to their favorite restaurant and order the same thing every single time, month after month, year after year. There's a big world out there!

Don't be afraid to get outside your bubble, whether it is about food, where you travel, or being open to meeting men in a new way. Many interesting and fascinating men are online, and they're waiting to meet you! The more time you put into finding a significant other, the sooner it will happen. One thing is for sure: spending your time watching TV or listening to your cat purr is not going to help you find the love of your life. Only learning the ropes and dedicating yourself to this new way of dating will make the difference. And remember, you can do all the reading and learning you want, but you must be proactive and *actually have dates.* At first it may seem overwhelming, but the more "practice" you get, the easier it becomes and the more relaxed, more confident you will be when meeting all kinds of men.

All kinds of men would include Archie, who I met at a local restaurant after we emailed a few times. He was an editor of some sort and because I like words, I agreed to meet him. It was not a good sign when he ordered a greasy appetizer for us, without asking, that I knew I would not like. After a few minutes he starting talking about his previous relationship...never a good idea. He said she was a narcissist, and they had just recently ended their eight-year relationship. I guess the most humorous thing he mentioned was that she was obsessed with black and white clothing; that was all she would wear. Consequently, he took her to South America to see penguins! Not making this up.

This was a "practice" date which was frustrating because it led me nowhere, but it still increased my ability to become more at ease meeting all types of men...introverts, extroverts, quiet, boring, charismatic, the list is endless. The mantra you will need to say to yourself after these "practice" dates is, "I will not give up, no matter what," *especially* when you are driving home in your car by yourself. Undoubtedly, you will meet the players, the selfish, the uninteresting, the emotionally unavailable... you get the picture. The only thing you must remember is that there are good, desirable men out there who want to find love and be in a caring, committed relationship...*just like you.*

Throughout this book, there will be constant reminders to not give up. Would it be worth your time to read something like, "Well, give it a few dates, months, or whatever, and if it doesn't happen, then you might as well throw in the towel." The belief that you can do it and find someone cannot help but move you in the right direction. When I first ventured into online dating, I wrote a simple sentence describing exactly what I wanted to happen and the specific traits my significant other would possess. Within a year and a half, everything I had written had come true.

This was not magic, voodoo, or wishful thinking. I knew I had to do what it would take to meet men and do something that was very scary and entirely out of my comfort zone. I had made mistakes and that is why I wanted to tell the story of my experiences. I want the best for other women who want to find the love of their lives. It does take effort, belief in yourself and confidence to make this happen. I see single women, and single men too, and wonder...are they happy? Maybe it is just my perception or my own lens that I look through, but many do seem wistful and more than likely would love to have a significant other in their lives. I guess a light bulb moment for me happened when a single, good friend of mine mentioned that she was lonely. I was shocked. Having been married for so many years, I didn't realize that even outgoing, involved people can and do get lonely. Most of them are reluctant to verbalize it, but loneliness has become an increasingly debilitating illness that can lead to anxiety and isolation in our society. Know that this can be overcome and one way is to find a significant other with whom you can share your life.

There will be ups and downs, but if you go on dates with the right attitude, the process can be enjoyable and be a positive learning experience. As long as you are open and accepting and believe in yourself and in the process, it can and will happen. *Believe this!* Not only can you gain experience and a better understanding of exactly the kind of person you want by going on numerous dates, you can also discover who you are and maybe figure out exactly why you aren't getting second dates.

Speaking of dates...this is a true story told by a bartender who witnessed the event. The guy was waiting at a table in a bar when the woman appeared carrying her cat. It was fairly obvious they were meeting for the first time (bartenders have a sixth sense about these dating scenarios). They weren't at the table long when the woman got up in a huff and left. Soon after the prospective match departed, the bartender went over and offered the guy, still sitting at the table, a drink on the house. Apparently, the woman could not find a sitter for her cat so she decided she would bring her cat along on the date. Question: who gets their cat a house sitter when they are gone for two to three hours?

Anyway, the guy she was meeting was somewhat taken aback and suggested that maybe the cat would be best on the floor instead of on the table between them. It was in a cat-carry cage so this was doable, but the woman became irate that anyone would even suggest her cat be on the floor, and so off she went. No second date here! There will be many that you like who don't like you back and those who like you that you know are not who you want. And then there will be those who sabotage any possibility of a future date by acting totally *crazy!*

8. "If It's Meant to Be, It Will Happen"

"Your significant other will show up when you least expect it." This is what many well-meaning friends may tell you. Sometimes it does work, an old high school flame at a reunion, etc. *But* if you want to find a significant other, you simply must be willing to be proactive and sometimes take the first step. Many women, and men too, would prefer to meet someone at the produce section of the local grocery store, at a community event, or possibly through a friend of a friend.

Does this ever happen? Of course it does...but realistically, your chances of finding a significant other online are much higher than seeing someone across a crowded room, meeting them, and knowing you will be together forever. We simply need to understand that the older

9

we get, the number of men who are available, unmarried, and men we would even consider dating will be much smaller compared to the number of men we would have come across when we were younger. This is not meant to scare you, but it is simply reality and needs to be understood. That is why online dating can fill a void as we realize we would like to meet someone whom we want to spend time with and have a relationship with that may end up being a long term one. Let's face it, taking the first step in many areas of life can be difficult. But many of us have learned that after taking that first step, it wasn't as frightening as we thought it would be.

Getting back to the produce section. Today, while grocery shopping, I saw a guy who worked in the produce section of my local store trying his hardest to get acquainted with a woman who was looking over the radish selection. As she walked by me after their encounter, I brazenly commented, "Who says you can't meet men in the produce section?" She laughed and said they realized they had worked together previously so they exchanged numbers. She looked very pleased. It happens! Just remember, it's the exception, not the rule. Realizing this, expand your horizons and don't be afraid to join what millions of singles are already doing.

Chapter 2—Dating and Other Scenarios

9. The Brain and Neuroplasticity

The brain is flexible! We *can* learn new things. We can learn to accept online dating even if it seems strange and not what we are accustomed to, it all depends on how badly you want *love*. The brain appears to accept and learn faster if things are repeated. It has been demonstrated by actual footage of neurons in the brain that they will connect and expand when we accept new and different activities we haven't experienced before. By repeating to yourself what you want, going beyond what you normally do, and thinking new ideas over and over, your brain is actually helping you connect to the reality of what you desire.

This is not fiction. It has been proven by scientific research. The adage, "You can't teach an old dog new tricks," is no longer true. Maybe we don't want to learn new tricks. But learning and believing and hence behaving in new ways, which we once thought was impossible, is now within our reach. It *is* possible to change our behavior and what happens in our lives by focusing on what we want and believing positive outcomes. Repetition is the key. Although repetition can become tiresome, whether reading it or thinking it, it does work when we want to change what we currently believe or think.

Believe in yourself and believe that you are deserving of love.

This is a common theme...it must be learned and believed if you want to meet someone. Write down exactly what you want and look at it every day. I know two sisters who had over one hundred qualities they desired in their "match." They laugh about it now, but one of them actually did meet the man of her dreams online. He had a friend who the sister eventually married. Think of all the qualities that you desire in a significant other. I'm not recommending one hundred! But have a few that are important to you. I don't think there is a magic number but I do believe it will help you as you meet new men. Just don't get obsessed with the idea that you have to have everything you *want* in a relationship. Try to figure out the innate qualities you *need* that are long-lasting. Dig deep and try to understand what is important to you.

What specific values are you looking for in a relationship? When you understand those that are important to you, you will be better able to assess the profiles you read. No one can tell you what specific traits to look for; only you can figure this out. The men I was initially attracted to would have a sense of humor, and who would write enough in their profiles to give a glimpse of what they did and what they enjoyed. It doesn't hurt to consider what physical attributes are important too—but be careful with this one. That good-looking man you may think you desire may treat you like last week's newspaper. It is surprising how certain physical attributes become less important when we find someone who is stable, vulnerable, and cares about us. Letting go of fear and being open-hearted doesn't hurt your chances either. Be cautious about setting limits on whom you want to love. Saying or believing you cannot accept anyone too old or too short or too far away may be getting you nowhere fast.

10. Letting Go of Fear

Perhaps wondering if you are worthy enough is the biggest challenge you will face along with the fear that accompanies most of our excuses. Fear is the underlying cause of why people give up trying to meet others in online dating. They will think of every excuse they can come up with instead of being truthful with themselves and realize they are afraid of the unknown. Trust me, if I can relinquish my fear and go flying with a stranger in a small plane, you can gather enough courage to meet someone at your local Starbucks for an hour, or at the very least email and start a conversation. Nothing ventured, nothing gained, right? Do whatever it takes to conquer your fears and step out of your comfort zone if you want to find happiness and love. "Life begins at the end of your comfort zone. So every time you get afraid...take a step forward"— Lionel Ritchie, American-singer songwriter.

You can learn all you can about online dating and have a good profile and good photos, but if your underlying belief is that it won't work and that you cannot stand this different way of meeting someone, chances are you will get your wish. It won't happen. So again...*believe, trust the process, and know you are worthy of love.* Remember, we usually get what we think we deserve. If you think highly of who you are and deserve only the best, you will probably meet those who feel the same. I have read many comments by women who want to find love, but their negativity is so overwhelming that their chances are negligible. Don't go down that negative path!

11. Too Much Information Too Soon

Let's deal with giving too much information too soon, with no filters, before we move on to picking a dating site that works for you. Revealing too much too soon is not productive.

For instance, there was Kyle...

I talked to him on the phone once to decide if I wanted to meet him. It was not a good conversation. He told me about the wife he had recently divorced, something uncomplimentary about her not meeting his needs. He also told me a horrific story that had happened to his family. I think it's good to give people a chance and realize that maybe they're nervous and unable to be themselves when they first have a conversation, but when they go way overboard, you will sense something isn't quite right.

Kyle wanted me to meet for coffee, but I suggested that he call again so we could have another conversation. Well, that apparently was not something he wanted to hear and he wrote me a long email about how he didn't think I believed what he had told me in our first conversation, in a very angry and accusatory tone. He then sent me another email and said he was not sure about "us." I didn't take the time to respond to tell him "there never was an 'us'" and would not be in the future! Why waste my time on an angry man who can't even deal with a request for a further chance to communicate?

12. When Rejection Is the Only Way Out

When you know it will not work, don't prolong things—just reject. Hopefully, you can do this with some empathy. Sometimes I think it is worth the time and effort to meet, but when we know immediately it just simply cannot ever be, there is absolutely no reason to pretend it might.

A Norwegian widower, Sven, who lived fairly close to me, kept emailing repeatedly, and even though I was suspecting it would not work, I gave him my number and we talked on the phone. He wanted to grab a bite to eat, so against my better judgment, I agreed to meet him. This is where sometimes you give a person who shows some interest a chance. I sincerely thought, he lives close-by and maybe if we enjoyed each other's company, we could be friends.

He spent most of the rather short evening talking about his deceased wife, her clothes, etc. His table manners also were not quite acceptable. That was the fastest meal I think I have ever eaten. I insisted I pay for my dinner and skedaddled right out of there. Speaking of— who pays when the server brings the check? Most dating experts say the man should, but women should also offer. This is undoubtedly a culture thing, but I'm not sure a big deal has to be made. Although I have to say, on a first date, most women may offer and then, if the man agrees to let her pay, she may have a little, (or a lot) of resentment for whatever reason. So perhaps splitting the bill would work for the first date. I felt, because of the circumstances, I would not feel comfortable expecting him to pay for mine simply because I knew I would not be seeing him again.

Back to the date: Why do some men insist on talking about their past love's clothes, alive or not? Maybe this is an anomaly but I had experienced it several times. Again, too much information too soon...or maybe just plain old information that no one is interesting in hearing? I did text him later to tell him I didn't think he was over her death. He still thought we were perfect for each other. Or was it his desperation?

I will return to some more of my dating experiences, but now to get to where it all begins...

Chapter 3—Picking the Dating Site

13. How to Find the Right Online Dating Site for You

A big site like Match, means more choices but also more competition. Match seems to cover the bases for all age groups. Or you may want to pick what they call a niche site such as OurTime or eharmony (for the over fifty and up singles); eharmony chooses matches for you based on your input. And there is Zoosk for seniors. These sites have fewer choices than a larger site like Match but also less competition which could be a positive factor. And there is JDate, for Jewish men and women who want to meet other Jewish singles. There is Coffee Meets Bagel, Tinder, Hinge, OKCupid and Bumble...which seem to work better for the twenties to forties set. And there is Elite Singles for those over fifty.

New dating sites seem to emerge/come-and-go on a regular basis and there are many; just pick one that meets your needs and that you're comfortable with. The online dating era is here to stay. It is probably best to choose a larger site or, if finances are not a problem, you can have a profile on two sites if you are willing to spend the time to make it worth your money. It's easy to find out all about the different online dating sites by going online and reading what singles think, and by researching the costs, etc. Most sites are fairly easy to use even for the unsophisticated tech user, so don't let that hold you back. I chose Match because it was easy for me to use and has a lot of profiles. Usually, the longer period of time you agree to pay their fees, the less expensive it will be per month. You can sign up for any length of time, (usually at least six months is good), and you can see if it works for you. If not, and you don't meet someone or at least communicate with someone in that time period, it's not difficult to pick another site and see if it fits your needs and possibly have even more choices to peruse. Argh...that sounds so cold. But it's reality.

The main thing to remember is it's not the site as much as how you use the site to your advantage. Putting time and effort into developing a good profile will be more important than your choice of dating site.

Chapter 4—Getting Started

14. <u>Steps to Getting Started</u>

Once you've decided on a site, review it and make sure you know how it works. Don't hesitate to call and talk to a customer representative if you have any questions. Having that option to talk to a customer representative can be helpful if you're having difficulty deciphering something you don't understand, especially if you aren't particularly tech-y. Basically, after doing what you need to do to sign up and write a good profile, then Match or whatever site you choose will send you matches as often as you want them in your inbox. The more you know about the dating site and the best ways to use it, the better equipped you will be to meeting suitable matches.

The usual sections, give or take a few, on a dating site are as follows:

- Photos
- Username
- Written profile
- Preferences
- Favorite places
- Reading list...books you have recently read
- Bucket list

15. The Most Important Categories

If a prospective match cannot get past poorly taken photographs and/or a written profile that is negative, uses bad grammar, misspellings, etc., they, (or you!) may have just missed someone whom they/you might have gotten to know. Men are very visual so they have to be at least somewhat attracted to your photos to take the time to email you. However, new statistics have revealed that sixty-four percent of people think common interests with someone is more significant than how they look. But you have to meet them first or at least have several phone calls before you can truly establish the common interests you may have. So the written profile may be more important, but photos will be the first view of you that prospective matches will see. This will be your first—and maybe last—chance to show your personality/looks in a positive, attractive way that makes men want to reach out to you before scrolling by your profile. It is of utmost importance that you look your very best to entice those who view your profile to contact you. First, let's get started on how to post good photos.

Chapter 5—Primary Photo

16. Women!! Photos are Important

The primary photo is the very first photo a potential match will see when looking at your profile. The primary photo is customarily a head shot without a hat or sunglasses, but I have seen primary photos with one or both of these accessories and they still looked good. If you have a primary photo with a hat or sunglasses, other photos you post definitely need to show you without them. Posting eye-catching and appropriate photos takes time. Don't try to rush choosing your photos, particularly the primary photo, as it will mean the difference between success and failure.

The most important thing to remember is to smile! Before even taking one photo that you might post in your profile, think about what you are doing. Make sure you and your life look enjoyable and that you are a happy person. *Smile* not only in your primary photo but in *every* photo. You will want to use the most flattering photo of you as possible for your primary photo and make sure it is current, usually within the past year. It wouldn't hurt to get a professional photographer, but make sure the professional photos aren't too stiff and formal. Having the same pose, wearing different clothes in an indoor setting won't cut it. Try to have the majority outdoors while doing an activity that is part of your life.

If you decide to take the photos yourself or have a friend take them, don't have wires in the background or other distracting obstacles. Avoid bathroom selfies or backgrounds that take away from your gorgeous self! It is imperative to post a good picture of *you* before they slide right by your profile. Bye! Of course, I broke the sunglasses rule, but it wasn't bad and I got some interest mostly because I looked like I was maybe twenty years younger. Is this why I got attention from the younger set? I have no idea how it happened; it was not photoshopped and was less than a year old when I used it. *But* I wouldn't recommend this because you want to use photos that look the most like you look currently. This is to prevent shock when you meet someone and they were expecting someone different than how you actually look. I heard a comedian on the radio recently who said things have gotten so bad with online dating with people saying how old they are and how old they actually are that he now requests they post a photo of themselves holding a current newspaper with the date on it.

17. Make Sure People Know Who *You* Are in Your Photos

I saw a primary photo of a man (and who I am assume was his deceased wife) who were kissing their granddaughter or daughter. They were posed on each side of her cheek. This was *his* primary photo. I have to say, I was surprised this got by his site's screeners or photo approvers. The primary photo should be a head shot of *you*—not added relatives or friends. The problem being: who is who? Is the profile about the daughter, the man, or the wife? It would be fairly simple to understand the man should be the focus, but why have three people when women looking at his photo are only interested in him? Normally, the dating sites will not approve more than one person in the primary photo, so this slipped by somehow. Unfortunately, if people who are viewing your photo, particularly your primary photo, can't figure out who is who, they'll swipe right by you.

Chapter 6—Other Photos in Your Profile

18. <u>Pick Six or Seven Other Good Photos, and a Full Body Shot Is a Must</u>

In selecting your photos, remember: no wedding rings, no hands belonging to someone else on your shoulder, no flowers (or at least not an overabundance of them). Use the very best photos you have of yourself in a variety of settings. You like hiking? Hiking is *big* in Seattle as is skiing, boating, kayaking, wine tasting and cycling...the list is endless. Whatever you enjoy doing, include a photo of you doing it! It shows you are out there enjoying life and not holed up in your home or apartment in your robe watching the latest hit series on TV.

For instance, since many men in Seattle are pretty much lumberjacks and do everything athletic there is to do (even older men in Seattle do all this healthy, athletic stuff). So if you live here, it wouldn't hurt to have a photo of you doing something active, like cycling, skiing, golf, even walking!—something to show you're still energetic and loving life. This is not just valid for Seattleites but everywhere. If you want a couch potato, fine, but most men and women are looking for someone who is active or at least attempts to be. I have an eighty-year-old female friend who bicycles around Mercer Island, a small island six miles from Seattle, almost weekly. If you aren't particularly busy, maybe it is time. I put a full-length photo of me with friends on a Segway tour in Seattle with a view of Mt. Rainier in the background. If you have decent balance and are fearless, this is great fun...almost ran over a tourist, but oh well.

19. Clothing: Know What to Wear!

Be conscious about what you are wearing. A dark heavy raincoat in Seattle is probably appropriate, especially in our eight months of winter, but I don't think it has much sex appeal. I made the mistake of wearing clothing styles too casual and even a flannel shirt or two. One guy from Sun Valley thought we were a perfect match because of the flannel and suggested we stop looking for anyone else after a couple of long distant phone calls. Seriously?!

20. Photos You Do Not Want

I recently saw a profile where the guy had a couple of cozy couch photos with his recently departed spouse. The next photo was of him and his deceased wife standing with their arms around each other. He then had another photo of what appeared to be him crying on his wife's sister's shoulder at his wife's memorial. Never, ever a good idea to post photos of anyone who is recently or not so recently departed. You can't make this stuff up. I wonder if he got many replies after posting these types of photos.

Evoking sympathy for whatever reason is never a good idea on a dating site. It reveals two things you may not want to project: one is that you aren't ready for a new relationship because you are still clinging, subconsciously or otherwise, to the past; or two, that you are not interested enough to take new, good photos that show what you look like and that you are ready to meet someone.

And then there are those men who will post a series of shots with their friends...all are approximately the same age and look similar. Who is who? Do you even want to try and figure it out? No! Swipe! I recently viewed a profile of a man with a beard. All of his photos showed him looking remarkably similar to the other men in the group photos he posted, all with beards and of similar stature. Who is who?! Are they attending a beard convention or what?

The same is true for posting photos of you with a group of your friends. Of course, you know who everyone is, but does that mean anyone else will? There is also a place to write a short sentence or a description about each photo you post so be sure to do this. Also, never post photos of yourself with the opposite sex unless they are family. I'm not even sure potential matches are interested in viewing your siblings and/ or your mom or dad. Maybe down the road, if you connect with someone, they will want to meet all of your family, but first they primarily want to see you. Many men appear to have the opinion that if they have photos of them posing with one or more scantily attired females this will somehow make them seem more attractive themselves. Instead, it is probably a huge turnoff for most women as it would be for men seeing a potential match with attractive male friends.

I don't know how many profiles of men I have viewed when researching for this book who write and/or post photos as if they don't have the energy or even care about looking presentable in their photos and/or the intelligence to tell even a little about who they are or something intriguing about themselves. Recently, I saw a seventy-year-old man's profile with bathroom selfies and him being shirtless while in the kitchen cooking...really? Maybe, if he's a thirty-year-old body builder— but these unflattering photos, something tells me, lead to absolutely nowhere.

21. Being Clueless About Photos

This is worth repeating. Don't be one of those people who take unflattering pictures and look like they are desperately in need of a shower... eewww. They wake up, stroll to the bathroom, and must think to themselves, "Hmm, probably as good a time as ever to take a selfie to post on that dating site." Don't be one of those thoughtless people who put such little effort into something. Note to any men who happen to read this: please look like you own a shaver and if you have a beard, put some attempt into making it appear somewhat presentable and *clean!*

Women of any age do not want to view let alone meet men, who look like they could care less how they come across in a primary photo. It also is very obvious that those online are not actively in search of a match when only one photo is posted. This does not reveal what anyone actually looks like and reduces chances of getting emails from others (see selfies, #22.) I have seen many men that look sooo unhappy...do they think this is appealing? Who wants to meet someone who doesn't have enough sense to even *try* and put a decent photo of themselves online and look as though they are at least relatively happy? There was one guy who, and I am serious, has had a picture of his not so slender stomach and his belt buckle as his primary photo for at least a month or longer, no legs or shoulders or head, just his very prominent stomach! Of course, he didn't do this on purpose...he was just so careless and clueless about technology.

This may be discouraging, but don't start believing you won't come across someone you find interesting and appealing to you. For all the slackers you will view, you will come across men who look good, or at least put some time into trying to look good, and have written a very thoughtful and detailed profile. I am telling you this because you need to know what you'll be up against when you go online. There will be many who have obviously put a lot of effort and time into their profiles; these are the prospective matches that will get the most emails. Make sure *you* are one of these people. Before you post your photos, have a friend look at all of them, so you can hopefully get an objective opinion that you are doing a variety of activities, and that you look happy, attractive, and at your best.

22. And Then Those Selfies

Okay, let's face it, we have entered the selfie era. *But* there are women and men on dating sites that do not know what they are doing. The photos are just bad. Sometimes it works, but photos taken by someone else or a photographer, as stated previously, will get you where you want to be a lot faster than posting not-so-attractive photos. Selfies and your background: please, please do not use bathroom selfies ever! Especially with underwear hanging on a hook in the background (a guy told me he actually saw this in a woman's online photo).

There are so many clueless men and women who take unbecoming selfies. It amazes me how many men's profiles I have viewed that have absolutely horrendous photos. I have used all of my will power not to email them and as politely as I can, tell them how to get their act together. It has been so tempting to let these clueless men understand they need to smile and dress appropriately by being fully clothed. A bathing suit is fine if they are pleased with their physique, but viewing someone lounging around half-naked is not appealing to most on a dating site.

The same goes for women. Don't assume a man wants to see you partially disrobed. Viewing photos will give you an idea of who is serious and who is not. Do they have one photo, taken in their bathroom? How much effort does that take? Not much. Don't waste your time on men who are half-heartedly trying, unless they have a written profile that is very appealing to you. If you are serious about meeting someone, do you want to take the time to communicate with a person who isn't putting any energy into coming across as truly committed to the process? People show how much they want to meet someone by revealing that they are willing to take the effort to post enough attractive photos and write a thoughtful profile to give others a glimpse into their lives and who they are. Think twice about emailing these unthinking matches who obviously would like to meet someone but reveal they have no energy in any way.

23. Other Photo No-Nos

To repeat, whatever you do, no photos of you with a man's arm around you, or a man in the photo at all! Again, no photos of your deceased spouse or photos of your past relationships. I recently saw a primary photo of a pilot in a cockpit—very enticing, except that he forgot to remove his wedding ring. And please, only one photo of you with your pet. Men are interested in you, not your pet, or other men. Having five pictures of your dog/cat is pretty much the same as a guy having five photos of fish! There are a lot of dog lovers out there so posting one is fine...we just sometimes have a problem keeping pet photos to a minimum.

24. So He Can Fish–But Is He a Great Catch?

For some unknown reason, many men think most women like viewing dangling fish. I've seen all sorts of fish and it puzzles me why men think this is something to behold. Don't be like these confused men who have photos that the opposite sex has absolutely no interest in viewing. Most men love fishing, and want to show off their catch; the bigger the better. But if the tables were turned, would they like to see photos of our make-up? If you *do* like fishing, definitely, by all means, have a photo of fish, dead or alive. Photos of fish will guarantee you get some interest. Or better yet, you watching a Seahawks or Mariners game or any sports anywhere in the country! Photos of you knitting or playing cards with your friends probably won't cut it.

25. Numerous Photos of Flowers and Sunsets

It has amazed me how many men post photos of flowers; they must be looking for a fellow gardener. Post good pictures of *you*; that is who others are interested in, and be sure to add captions and dates by each photo. It doesn't hurt to have a photo of you with some friends as long as they aren't better looking than you! To repeat, make sure that who-ever looks at your profile knows who you are in each photo. If you have grandkids, that works; just don't put more than one with your darling little namesake(s). And adding a photo or two with your kids or your grown children is a positive idea too. When people over-post photos of everyone and everything else except them, it shows a certain lack of confidence. Yes, it's good to have a variety, but remember they are primarily interested in *you* and not your family or all the other people in your life.

26. Most Importantly!

You do not have to be a beauty queen or thirty-five to find true love. If you have confidence and a good personality, remember this: some men will find you attractive even if you don't have a perfect hourglass figure. Not all men are shallow and care only how you look. *Believe in yourself* and when you do, and don't give up, you can and will find someone. Again, people usually get what they think they deserve. As stated previously, be sure to include a full body shot of you...this is crucial. Honesty is always the best policy and cannot be overstated, so have good photos but also ones that look like you—the *whole* you.

Not every man is looking for a thin woman. Many men, especially if they weigh a little more, actually want to find more curvaceous women. Do not think you have to lose that last ten or fifteen pounds or even thirty! I have a good friend who is divorced and approaching sixty. She thinks she weighs too much to try online dating. She has a wonderful personality and actually a good figure, but doesn't understand that *now* is the perfect time for her to give it a try. You never know, a few extra pounds could be an asset and attract the man of your dreams. There are good men out there and then there are others like...

27. Robert

Ah yes, Robert...close to seventy years old and standing in front of numerous law books looking extremely dignified. His age range of who he wants? Women from thirty-five to fifty. When I was back in my Midwestern home town and showing my friends the selection of men on Match, we ran across Robert's profile and decided to send him an email: "This is a dating site, not an adoption site." Not nice, but after a few drinks, we had a good laugh. Can you even imagine a seventy-year-old woman looking for a thirty-five-year-old man!? In reality, our culture is fine when men search for much younger women, so in all fairness, if you find someone much younger and if it works for both parties, I'd say go for it!

28. Honesty with a Capital H

As stated previously, honesty is always the best policy. One quote I like is, "Honesty saves everyone's time"—Anonymous. No need to backtrack and try to remember what you said. Honesty can make you vulnerable, but isn't honesty what most people are seeking? When you are completely honest about your height, weight, or anything else, you won't have to apologize down the road for making something up that wasn't the truth. There are exceptions to this rule. I had a friend who said she was five years younger than she actually was. Later, when the truth came out, her new significant other was happy because he wanted her to be closer to retirement age so they could travel. They are now happily married and travel all over the world.

There are those who post a younger age for the sole purpose of not wanting to be overlooked based on a number. That can work as long as you do end up telling how old you are—maybe on a second or third date?

29. Way Back When

Do you seriously want to see baby pictures of a prospective match? Cute, adorable grandkids are one thing, but please!—no baby photos of you. It can be okay to put a younger version of you if you make it clear how long ago it was and if it is interesting. For instance, if you were the baby model for Gerber baby food, that might be acceptable. *Make sure all of your photos have a date* or at least the year it was taken. This needs repeating because people forget to do this and it is a mistake. Again, when you meet for a first date, there should be no surprises.

30. Dated Photos

I have seen many men who post old photos of themselves, or a photo that looks like it was taken with a Kodak Brownie camera eons ago. They usually have a yellowish tinge to them, which is a dead giveaway. If they are that out of touch, why bother? Don't go back into your shoebox and dig out those dated photos. No one cares how we looked years ago. It's as if they think, "Gee, I looked pretty good back then so maybe that will stir up some curiosity." Never mind that they weigh one hundred pounds more now than way back when. Yoo-hoo...reality check. Most of us looked better ten, fifteen, or thirty years ago! And then there are those who post photos from all different eras of their lives. Make sure you don't look like completely different people. I have viewed profiles and have found it shocking. "Wait, it looks like there are five different people in this profile." Are they totally oblivious to how this appears? Again, make sure people know who *you* currently are and what *you* look like today.

31. Photos Continued...

Don't post twenty! But post enough, maybe five to seven, that will give the viewer different sides of you. And again, clothing is important. Tight clothing revealing most of your body will result in men who are mostly interested in that aspect and will be the ones reaching out to you. If you want a long-lasting relationship, try to appeal to men who are interested in who you are, not just your body. Most of us understand that sexual chemistry and physical attractiveness can take us just so far and then...poof! The connection is gone.

We do want to be appealing physically and that is why you must try to have visually attractive and appropriate photos. However, overtly sexual photos are *not* a good idea. Sexual chemistry cannot, nor should not, be denied, but clothes that are outdated and reveal waaay too much may not be how you want to come across. I once saw a current photo of a guy I had corresponded with dressed in what appeared to be clothing styles from the Fifties. You probably want to refresh your wardrobe if your clothes are that old. This is where a good friend or two can give you a true viewpoint, if you ask for their honest opinion.

If you are actively involved in something, put a photo of that included in your profile. I once put a photo of me standing by a Maserati convertible at a high-end local mall, University Village, in my profile. I didn't pretend it was mine but still got a lot of interest from car buffs. I am not into cars, so I removed this photo. But if you particularly like something, be sure and include it, especially if you would like to meet someone who has the same common interest.

Chapter 7—Your Username

32. Pick a Catchy Username

This is the name that will go under your primary photo. I mistakenly used the name of my dog because I didn't realize it would be front and center and just picked something I wouldn't forget. So happy my dog's name is not Fido or Buddy! Something catchy usually gets attention. For someone named Bob, 'What About Bob?' is kind of clever or how about 'Ken—looking for Barbie'. Most women don't think they want to be Barbie...so this guy may have to explain it was for humor only and not really what he wants a woman to be–or look like! At least it could be a conversation starter. Choosing an attention-grabbing username may take a bit of thinking to come up with, but it's worth it. This is fairly important because it is one of the first things that catches our eye when perusing potential matches, along with the primary photo. Personally, I would usually just skip someone with a username that was dumb, corny, or boring. Match has recently converted to using actual first names or a nickname so you are ready to go on that site. I see nothing wrong in using your real name with a few numbers to distinguish yourself from the 150,000 other Lindas, Susans, or Pams.

Chapter 8—Written Profile: Telling Who You Are

33. The Profile is *You!*

Okay, now that you have some decent photos, try writing the most positive things about yourself and what you want in a relationship. You'll want to write three or four well-written paragraphs. This will determine if you get any replies. Staying positive and using words like "love," "fun," "caring" is usually the best route to take. Most men want to spend time with someone who likes to laugh and who they feel good around. When you come across as Debbie Downer, it's kind of...well...a downer. Mention things *you want*, not what *you don't want*. Don't write something that is inauthentic; most people can sense when something is being fabricated. Men want to reach out to someone who comes across as genuine and believable.

Make sure you let the reader know what you are currently involved in, what you want to do, and include some stories about what you have done. I read once where a woman put a question in her profile asking for help deciphering her Lexus manual because she couldn't understand how to set her windshield wipers. Having a Lexus myself, she was not making this up as it has taken me about three years to try and figure that one out! She got so many emails from men it was astonishing. So be creative and come up with whatever problem men can't help but want to solve!

If you have trouble writing an appealing profile, seek help. Maybe you know a friend who has better writing skills and can improve your profile. There are even professional profile writers out there, so don't be hesitant to hire them. But don't pay them anything unless you know they have written profiles for your age range, because if they are gearing your profile toward the forty-and-under age group, it just won't work, primarily because every generation has its own understanding of our culture. Everyone loves reading stories! Try your hardest to tell a story around something you have recently done or accomplished. This may take some time and effort, but is worth it because you can bring the reader into your life and give them an idea about who you are. Consider writing something funny or amusing that happened to you. Revealing who you are and being vulnerable in this way can attract and make men want to contact you.

A word of caution: be careful about going overboard and telling every little detail of how wonderful you are and how great your life is. I recently read a profile of someone's travels; what a wonderful career they have had, their terrific children and grandchildren, how healthy they are and how well they "clean up." They ended their profile saying they are looking for someone who looks good, is healthy, and well-traveled like them. There is something to be said for being self-assured but be aware of how this can come across.

34. Skipping Over Profiles

Don't rush and go online without a decently written profile. Decently written means good English, or in whatever your native language is. No misspellings and/or incoherent paragraphs. I am kind of a freak when it comes to spelling and usually can't forgive poor grammar or misspellings unless they misspell hors d'oeuvres...or concierge...ha. What I find most curious are men who profess to have PhDs and cannot write a simple paragraph without grammatical errors and misspellings.

Proofreading is important because when you don't, there are things which will be written unintentionally. Not a huge problem but again, why come across as someone who cares half-heartedly about their profile? Examples of when people didn't take the time to read what they have written—funny, but annoying, too: "...don't play games as we are of age unlike the young guts out there," "Right now I am reading Bibble," and "I like to meet a lady any place with lots of free parking." One small grammatical error in this last example, but I found this hilarious. Can't wait to meet this guy! Bet he wants me to pay for the coffee, too. And then I saw "Right now I am reading movies." The one that was extraordinary was, "My wife died three years ago and I am looking to replace her." Had to read that one several times to make sure a guy actually wrote this—you can't make this stuff up.

35. Write About Yourself

Never, ever, and I repeat, never, post anything regarding your past status or particularly anything about a deceased spouse. (The exception being where it requires you to state if you are divorced, widowed, never married, etc.) You can do this later if you develop a solid relationship and you both are comfortable revealing things from your past. This is not, however, something you want to do until you have established a connection...preferably in person. Oh, and be wary of those who are currently separated. Do you really want to go there?

36. Ditch the Past, Especially When You Meet in Person

Sam was an architect who lived on Bainbridge Island, a quaint community thirty-five minutes by ferry from Seattle. He previously owned a sailboat and obviously knew how to sail. I emailed him because I was interested in sailing. We thought of a few different things to do but decided to go on a sailing charter on Lake Union, a small lake in the heart of Seattle. We would meet at a restaurant close by and then join some good friends of mine.

During the brief time we talked and had appetizers, he told me about the tragic death of his daughter and how he and his wife had consequently divorced afterwards. This is way too much information you want to tell someone you've just met. We were not a good match which I figured out during the rest of the evening, but he texted me when I got home and wanted to get together again. In hindsight, and because I want to treat others the way I want to be treated, I should have texted him back but I didn't respond. He probably figured out something was awry when I jumped into my car after our date and took off as quickly as humanly possible when the valet arrived!

37. Avoid a Generic Profile

List some of the characteristics of the man you want. The more specific you are, the closer you will get to the attributes you want. Try also to give a thoughtful view into who you are and how your friends would describe you. Keeping your written profile to 150 to 300 words is good. Don't feel you need to write a novel. But *again*, remember everyone likes stories. Additionally, ending with something romantic is something that can catch a fellow romantic.

38. Mother Figures

I have had serious email inquiries from guys in their thirties. (Perhaps looking for a mother they never had or someone who they thought would take care of them?) My reply was always the same: "Really? You're younger than my son!" My one exception was from a very attractive, young guy. I actually think he was for real because he emailed me several times and wanted to meet. I told him I would meet him at Starbucks only if we could make sure my daughter showed up at the same time and I introduced him as "This is my new boyfriend." What was that old Mastercard slogan? "Priceless!"

Before moving on, the following is the profile I put on Match:

> We both love to laugh but we'll also have a serious side and have meaningful conversations about our world and what is important to both of us. We have good ideas about what to do and see in Seattle...and do them together. We will undoubtedly bring out the best in each other and care about each other's extended families. The man I choose is caring and kind, open-minded and active...and romantic. He will know who he is and have self-confidence. One of his favorite sayings is I can do that. He has a passion not only for life but other things he cares about, and wants to share them with...me! We both have things we do independently, but prefer spending time together when we can. Honesty and trust are understood by both of us. Would prefer dating someone close to my age-but does age matter when we find love/chemistry and passion? Most of my friends consider me open to adventures, a nature lover (take spiders outside instead of the opposite), an environmentalist, and generous. Most years were spent going to and from horse shows. The majority of my free time, when not trying to convince a horse to get into a trailer, was spent working for the environment with friends and for non-profits. The Pacific Northwest is so beautiful, it reminds us daily why we need to protect what we have left. Currently working on a fundraiser to benefit an environmental group of which I am a board member. Coming from the Midwest and raised in a small town, I feel dating has changed, particularly as a some-what recent widow, but still believe in chances for love. Just returned from Hawaii, and have plans to visit Boston with seven friends from elementary school this fall and have a sailing cruise in the San Juan Islands planned for August.

Want to do what requires fearlessness (is that a word?). Now that I have the time...would like to do some hiking, learn how to sail, and do those things that we both enjoy. Hope that includes sitting in front of a fire and toasting to us!

I have included this personal profile to reveal that it wasn't perfect but I thought it said what I wanted it to and it did attract some feedback and first dates. Some of the men I've had first dates with included several CEOs, a professional photographer, an editor, an entrepreneur, and a previous commander of a submarine. I emailed back and forth and had conversations with a prominent land attorney and a trial attorney. I am attracted to confident, intelligent men because they are interesting and have achieved success in their lives. The one thing I did learn in this process is, if you want a secure, confident leader as your partner, you better be willing to let them take the lead. So be careful what you wish for because you may just get it!

Chapter 9—Preferences

39. Distance: How Far Are You Willing to Travel to Meet Someone?

This is absolutely up to each individual. If you don't mind dating long distance by all means include your distance range—all the way from where you live to NYC and back. However, if you are like me...been in Seattle traffic lately? I wanted someone within thirty miles. And I understood this would greatly limit the number of prospective men I would be able to choose.

But research has shown that the closer you live to someone, the better the chances of a relationship forming. You can choose a shorter distance and then expand it later if there aren't many men around you. Distance also means the longer the drive, the more time you need to have to do that drive. I have many friends who are fifteen years younger than I am who are terrified of driving in our increased traffic, so traffic is something to consider. Men and women are working much longer than they used to, or so it seems. If they are working forty hours a week and then have other responsibilities and you work as well, this could likely affect how often you get to see each other. But if you are particularly brave, love to drive, travel, and aren't hesitant, the world is your oyster.

40. Make a List of Whom You Want

Before even writing your profile, consider making a list of exactly who you want to date. A good idea is to have written something and have it in your subconscious. Not just physical attributes, but core values that are important to you–maybe kindness, interest in the world, generosity, the list is endless. Many dating gurus will suggest you do this. This isn't something you should have to put in your profile but it certainly wouldn't hurt if you reveal what kind of person you would like to have in your life. Internalizing *and* stating what kind of values you want will attract those who have similar beliefs and values as you.

41. Zero In

So who do you want to meet? Someone your own age? Someone younger, older? The wider the age range, the more choices you will receive as matches. Remember again, in our culture, it is quite acceptable for men to not only date much younger women but to seek them out. It's a double standard but it is what it is and probably won't be changing anytime soon. An acceptable range is ten years; five years younger and five years older. But this is a personal choice. If you are fifty and don't mind dating older men, put your age range as high as you want.

I learned of a recent widower, who, upon approaching sixty-five, is now seriously involved with someone a year older than his daughter, who is forty-one. This happens frequently, and who is to judge? When you're in your forties and early to mid-sixties, you will get many responses from older men! When you're in your upper sixties and seventies and eighties, the available men are a smaller number due to the simple fact that men don't live as long as women, *and* most men, not all, prefer dating younger women. So be as flexible as you feel you can...it will increase the number of men with whom you will be matched. I preferred dating men my own age, maybe a year or two younger up to five or six years older, and that worked for me. But I was happy to hear from a girlfriend recently who is fifty-eight and is dating a thirty-three-year-old man. I say good for her—and him!

42. More Preferences

There's a whole bunch of agnostics and atheists in Seattle and presumably everywhere. If you want someone of your own faith and it is significant to you, you can state your religion...just remember, the less rigid you can be with all of your preferences, the more men you will see as matches. You do want to check widow or divorced or separated or never married so they will know what your status is. A big no-no is trying to go on a dating site while you're married. Being separated is apparently okay, but married? One guy who emailed me several times said he was about to give up when he saw my profile. It sounded way too fishy so I did some research, and he was married! Wonder if his wife appreciated this...had she known. If you encounter this, do other online daters a favor and report it to your dating site.

Moving along, you'll want to fill in your choice of physical preferences: body type, age, everything about you (you give a description of your characteristics), and whom you want to meet. A friend of mine insisted her husband must be at least six feet tall and he turned up magically on her Match search. They are now happily married with two children. So if there are some characteristics you must have, then go for it. The Universe does provide!

Speaking of the Universe, there are many men and women who are doubtful that it will provide much of anything. But as I've aged, I have read and heard many stories of people who have overcome obstacles in their lives and become successful in what they dreamed of because of what they believed could happen. Did it take action and the willingness to be determined and go outside of their comfort zones, including time and effort, to make their dreams come true? Yes, it did. But without the underlying belief that the Universe will provide, who knows the outcome? Your belief that all things are possible will not hurt your chances of finding love.

43. Dealbreakers

We all have dealbreakers. All it takes is some thought for you to figure out what yours are, whether it's alcohol, smoking, etc. If these are deal breakers for you, you can check "No Way." State what you want and look for people who state what they want. This is what a match is all about; finding a significant other who shares your common goals, values, interests and likes.

Some men post in their profiles that a good time consists of watching TV, relaxing on their favorite couch. Most men *and* women do not seek out boring people who have little or no hobbies or interests, who are mostly tuned into a game show or a reality show on TV, or who actually state, "I like hanging out at home with my remote on the couch...care to join me?"

I'm not making this up, but who knows? Maybe this would appeal to a certain percentage of online daters. (You have to give it to them; at least they're honest!) Believe it or not, I have read many profiles that say something like, "Looking for someone just to do things with," and maybe one other short sentence. If you are easy to entertain and like simplicity, by all means go for it, but does it sound captivating at all?

Politics is another hot topic today. I have an older, one-time married, close friend who decided to break up with the true love of her life she met after her divorce because their politics did not match. Only afterwards did she realize what a mistake this was because they were so well matched in all other areas. Unfortunately, this was a regret that could not be remedied.

There is much you can decipher by what both men and women write in their profiles; by what is said and what is left unsaid. Do you want to spend your time emailing someone who cannot put together even a few paragraphs describing who they are? And then there are those who go the opposite direction, listing all about their travels and everywhere they had stayed and what they did. Again, remember to write what is interesting and gives a clue into who you are and what your life is like. Just don't go overboard, and try not to compliment yourself with something like, "I have a beautiful smile," even if you do. Another popular one is, "I look much younger than I am." Let others be the judge of that. Humble is good.

44. Believing

If you don't truly believe in the possibility of your finding love and are making a half-hearted attempt, but subconsciously thinking it's a waste of time, nothing will likely happen. "You get what you think you deserve." I love this quote because it's so true. If you think there is no one on the planet who you will like or who is good enough, you are probably right. There are admirable men and women, like you, who are seeking companionship and love. Tap into those neurons and believe it can happen. Maybe you will find a true person you care for immediately, but usually it takes some time to find someone with whom you are compatible. *Believe in love* and have the confidence and perseverance to get what you want.

45. The Illusion of Perfection

When we are looking for love, we sometimes expect the men we meet to have everything our heart desires and then some. This is not only unrealistic but will limit your chances of meeting a caring partner because they cannot ever meet your expectations. Don't take this path. The desired height, wealth, education, etc., of someone might be what you think you must have to be in love, but occasionally, when you meet someone who adores you and cares deeply about you, you may realize that this is ultimately more important than their bank account or certain physical traits.

Even things in their past that you thought you would never be able to accept can be overcome. This is not "settling." It is realizing that love can exist without the conjured images of what we believe we need to be in a relationship—or what others tell us we need or should have. When we are able to accept someone who can reveal their true soul to us, anything is possible. This is especially important as we age. Most of us have issues that we have moved beyond. This is okay. When we can accept ourselves as we are, we can also accept others more easily. This is not only true spiritually but physically as well. Many of us feel we are still twenty-five, in both spirit and body, but unfortunately, gravity produces bodies that aren't quite what they used to be. Plus, those who age gracefully and are accepting and honest about who they are, shows us their vulnerability, which is something that we all want in a mate.

Chapter 10—Other Personal Details

46. <u>Favorite Places</u>

It could be a country, a national park or even a restaurant—the sky is the limit. This gives others who are looking at your profile a view into your life. Again, please don't talk about every place you have traveled, exotic or otherwise, in the last twenty years. Not everyone is interested in an obscure building in Timbuktu. Superfluous details about travels and unwanted information is not what people want to know. They want to know about *you!*—not where you have traveled every year of your life. This is so tedious for those reading your profile. Mention a *few* fascinating places you have traveled to in the last five years and call it good. And mentioning places you want to go is always a good idea...who knows? Someone you might enjoy may have similar travel desires.

Restaurants are good too. Name a few local hotspots that are popular...they might also love the same place. Weaving a story around a travel experience or even your everyday life will give a clue into who you are and what your life is like. Again, people love stories! Especially ones that are humorous.

47. <u>Recent Books You Have Read</u>

Be truthful. If you list a few books you have not read and then they ask you later in person or on the phone what you liked about the book and you don't have a quick and thoughtful answer, well...that's not good.

This doesn't happen often but it can. So hopefully you have some books you have read recently. It will give the person reading your profile some insight into who you are. There will be times when you know immediately that the person would not be a good match for you by what they like to read. For instance, *Guns & Ammo* (does this publication even still exist?) would be a quick turnoff for me...yet maybe some of you wouldn't be offended by this interest.

48. Bucket List and Final Review

How adventurous are you? Your bucket list can give people a clue about how adventurous you are. Try not to have too many but enough to show what intrigues you and what you really want to do. If you are an adrenaline junkie and like high-energy activities, this could be very attractive to a fellow sky diver! Or even watching sky divers! We all have different energy levels; men and women today do every activity imaginable even up into their eighties. The trick is to find someone who is compatible with your energy level. Just be honest and include things you would like to do or even things you have done previously but want to share with someone.

49. After Filling in All the Blanks

Double check your profile before going online!—particularly the photos and written profile. Make absolutely certain that you have been honest with current photos and don't fudge when it comes to weight, height, or education, etc. The truth will come out eventually and it's better to be honest from the very beginning. Honesty always pays in the long run. Statistics have shown that men online exaggerate their income while women like to shave a few—or many!—pounds off their true weight—and age. This isn't really a good idea, because the truth usually reveals itself sooner or later, and then prospective matches lose respect for you and the whole process. If you are "curvaceous" then go with that. This goes back to posting photos. When you have photos of you thirty pounds lighter and then show up looking a bit (or a lot) heavier, things usually don't go well. I know from experience what it is like when you are meeting a person and they look like someone else. No surprises, please! The written profile needs to be reviewed too. Don't post something that is not who you are and inauthentic. It's a good idea to have a friend read your profile to give you, hopefully, an honest opinion of how you come across and maybe catch any typos.

Chapter 11—Initial Contact

50. Ready to See What Happens

So you've picked a site and have downloaded some good photos, and a truthful, positive, and hopefully humorous written profile. You've checked your preferences and are going to see what happens. Most men will want to meet you as fast as they can so they can visually assess you and see if you meet their expectations. This was one of the things I learned since I started dating. Men are different than women. I knew this; I just didn't realize how much different. Maybe that difference is why we love them.

Still, there is something to be said about talking on the phone first. I don't have too many rules, but this is one. I absolutely will not meet someone I have not talked to on the phone. You can tell more than you need to know after a few conversations and decide if you want to take your time getting ready and driving to meet them. If they don't want to, don't have the time, etc., to spend an hour talking before meeting you, assume they really are not that into you *or* as mentioned, have to see the goods before spending any time conversing or getting to know you. If you are bored and enjoy going on short coffee dates and don't mind taking the time to meet someone in a safe environment, by all means do it! This is a judgment call.

I want to know if I can relate to someone and will intuitively know after talking to them whether or not I want to meet them. If you enjoy meeting new people and have extra time and energy, arrange for a get together and see what happens. Meeting all kinds of men will give you an idea of whom you enjoy. And it might give you more confidence in the dating realm. But beware: a friend once told me she had a girlfriend who had been on five hundred coffee dates. Seems like she's made a career out of this...in other words, the "serial dater." I think she's still looking. Don't get caught up with only having short coffee dates and believing the idea that you are actually getting to know someone. If you are sincere and you are truly looking for someone to be involved with, it is doubtful this approach will get you where you want to be.

51. Talking on the Phone

Does the conversation flow and do you like what they say? Or, do they talk the entire time about themselves and never ask anything about you or your life? Do they make you laugh or, are they like Larry, who was so funny in his short emails, but on the phone was negative and went on a rant about his neighbor's dogs, and just seemed somewhat unpleasant. I went against my better judgment and drove and took the time to meet him. Let's just say between his flirting with the server and his lack of manners, it was a short evening. Plus, he did not appreciate my sense of humor. I texted when I arrived and said, "I am the best-looking woman in the parking lot." Of course, later I did tell him I was the only person in the entire lot. He didn't find it funny.

Bob looked good on paper but on the phone, uh oh. His first emails centered around poetry. I had just written my first poem and he said he wrote poetry too and we could get together and look at the five hundred poems he had written. Whew, wears me out just thinking about that. Anyway, we did end up talking on the phone and all he could say was "yes" after everything I said. How could a trial attorney have such a small vocabulary? Was he exhausted from using so many words in his poetry? He wanted to get together but I said "no"! It is important to give everyone a chance, especially when they appear nervous, but when you know it simply will not work, you must reject!

I connected with David, a physician, and he talked an entire one hour and a half about all of his joint replacement surgeries (his body, not of his patients) and his kids. He lived a long distance from Seattle but was anxious to drive up so we could meet. At the risk of sounding pretentious and overly judgmental, I realized that his car, clothes and home were straight from the Sixties. Having already lived through the Sixties and a great time it was!—I just saw no need to revisit that era. After one more conversation, not unlike the first, I thought to myself, "No thanks, think I would rather stay home and clean my tile."

No one will ever tell you to do what I did in the following situation: I thought I would really like Alan and loved his recent (so he said) photos. We spent probably at least forty hours talking on the phone. We didn't live very close to each other and he worked full time so we just kept having regular phone conversations and texting back and forth. I did it for one reason...he made me laugh. Because we had such long conversations and felt comfortable with who we each were, we decided to meet at my home. It was in the afternoon and I felt perfectly safe, but it was just too awkward. I couldn't just get up and leave to go home because I *was* home. What happened next was not good...keep reading.

52. Dishonesty

When you pretend to be who you are not, it usually doesn't work. I loved talking to Alan but I knew when we met, he could not have aged ten years in a month and a half...at least that is what appeared to have happened. So, when someone asks you if your photos are recent, be truthful. His age wasn't the only thing that didn't work for me, but it did change my perception of who he was. Always tell the truth! It will work to your advantage. Without truth, love doesn't happen, at least in my experience. I contacted him several months later because of the guilt

I felt after our first date. He figured out by my actions on our first date that a second date wouldn't be happening—the chemistry we had on the phone unfortunately did not happen in person, at least for me. All was good and I felt relieved and glad I had done that. Remember, karma is alive and well. It pays to treat people the way you want to be treated.

53. How Long to Wait Before Meeting in Person

This is absolutely up to you. Ninety-nine percent of dating coaches will tell you to meet as quickly as possible. But once in a while, (depending on the personalities and histories of the two people who have connected, and particularly now during a pandemic), it may just work if you both want to really know someone before meeting. The following is a true story: A forty-five-year-old man talked/emailed/texted with a thirty-eight-year-old female for three months before meeting. This was the nephew of a good friend of mine. Neither had been married previously. When they did meet it was *love*. They have since married and are very happy. Sometimes advice is good but other times, go with what you feel is best for *you*!

Chapter 12—Before Pressing "Send"

54. <u>Texting, Texting, Texting!</u>

If you don't have a smart phone and don't know how to text, get one and learn how to text *now*. Believe it or not, there still exist people, men *and* women *today,* who still use flip phones and take five minutes to send a text. Texting is our new form of communication. It shouldn't be the only way you communicate, but it is here and here to stay. It's fast, easy and can reveal a lot about the person you are connecting with... plus your kids and grandkids will love you for it. Remember, emojis are good; just don't overdo it. Some people seem to think if one emoji is good, then why not fifteen or twenty? In one text message! Remember, less is more. Once you start texting, you will undoubtedly send a text to the wrong person if you're texting two or more people at one time, so the general rule is: *check before sending*—which leads me to:

55. <u>Jack</u>

Initially, I thought we were a perfect match; he was close to my age, we spoke easily on the phone and we had a few common interests. We did have a difficult time deciding on a time to meet. I had a full schedule, then he had to cancel due to an unexpected meeting. Some things happened during our initial conversations on the phone that I questioned, but during one conversation we arranged to meet later that same day only to have him text me in an hour to say that he once again couldn't make it. A few minutes later, I received a text from him saying "shorts"—and yes, it was one of the rare, beautiful, sunny days we have in Seattle. Hmm...he just broke a date with me a third time, and now I'm inadvertently getting a text from him that he meant to send to someone else. It doesn't take a genius to figure out what was happening. He texted me shortly afterwards and said "Disregard previous text." Would he be telling his business associates to wear shorts? No. Would he be telling his adult children to wear shorts? No. Would he be telling his golfing buddies to wear shorts? No. Would he be telling a date to wear shorts? Yes! But every intuition I had I threw out the window. Trying not to make assumptions that he had broken our date because he found a better prospect, I still went to meet him a few days later. (More about that shortly.)

One of my friends asked me what Plan B is as it pertains to online dating. Plan B means you are second choice...when first choice doesn't work, then maybe you will work as a second choice. I will not be Plan B ever! At least not when I know I am plan B! (We are occasionally Plan B when we don't know we are Plan B...sometimes that works.) We can't expect people we are interested in to stop making plans with everyone, *but* when you know you are Plan B and know they are not respecting you or your time, you must reject!

I actually had a clueless man email me and say, "I am meeting someone at 1 p.m. [that someone being a prospective match]. Would you like to come and meet me at 3 p.m.?" We're talking same day, same location! I replied, "So thoughtful of you! But no, I am not applying for, nor wanting a job interview, and oh by the way...I will not be Plan B." Some of this stuff you can't make up.

Back to Jack. When someone tells you who they are, *believe them!* Jack owned a plane (complete with its own parachute—they actually manufacture these), a fifty-foot sailboat, and was charming, good looking, and very intelligent. What's not to like? He climbed mountains, did extreme skiing, went scuba diving, sailed, and flew everywhere conceivable. During the brief lunch we eventually did end up having, Jack proceeded to pull out his phone where he read off his bucket list of twenty-six places he wanted to visit. He talked about places I had never even heard of.

I'm pretty sure he was looking for a Wonder Woman who could do all of this and more, plus maybe a gourmet cook wearing nothing but an apron? In hindsight, I so wish after receiving the "shorts" text I would have replied back, "Maybe it would be better if we just forgot about getting together." After realizing I was not Wonder Woman, (nor could I be or want to be, at least not in this lifetime), he ate as quickly as he could and that was it. I did learn something from our encounter, however. It occurred to me that he had "destination addiction" (believe it or not, I first heard this term used by a Buddhist monk in a class I had taken). In other words, he always wanted to be somewhere where he wasn't. He told me briefly about his very painful divorce including an affair his wife had, from which I felt he had not recovered. The only thing I could think of was this: "Wherever you go, there you are." When you are not at peace within yourself, you will always be searching for someone, something, or somewhere else that will fulfill you and you will undoubtedly seek perfection or a duplicate of someone who broke your heart.

Chapter 13—First Dates

56. How Do We Arrive at a First Date?

A couple of thoughts: if you sit back and wait for them to email you, you are wasting time! If you see someone you're interested in and like what they've written, don't hesitate to send them an email. The dating rules have changed. Men like to be approached first. If they are not interested in you they will either give no response or will send you a short email saying they aren't. This is how online dating works! Move on, there are others who will respond.

But you may ask how do you exactly figure out who you think you would potentially like? You must be somewhat attracted to them physically but try not to be overly particular. Remember, their personality may be one that you love. If you don't give them a chance to even meet you, you may have swiped by someone who could turn into a significant other. Their looks will normally be what attracts you first, followed by what they write. If they don't write much of anything and have a sentence or two similar to, "I like to ride my motorcycle on the weekend and like hiking too," and it fits your lifestyle and is okay with you, then I would say at least email them to get a conversation started. This is a personal choice we all have to make. I would not be interested in someone who posts one picture and writes one sentence in his profile, but we all look for different things we want in a match.

The dating gurus will tell you to look for what you need, not what you want. What we may want is Prince Charming, but will Prince Charming stick around when you're in the fifth day of a head cold and can barely get out of bed? Plus, not exactly looking like Cinderella? The attributes of kindness, caring, empathy, and a giving nature may be more of what we need if we are thinking of a long relationship. These values would seem to override someone who thinks more of themselves than you. This sometimes takes a while to understand when relationships first begin. But your intuition and their actions will tell you if you are number one or number five in their list of priorities. It constantly amazes me when I read of women who know the men they are dating are not what they want or need but they refuse to make the break and hang on way too long. Our days are limited on this planet. Let go and move on!

When you have corresponded and eventually get to the point of meeting, believe it or not, first dates can be fun. They may lead to a second date...or not. If not, don't become discouraged. Remember, you could meet someone on your next get-together that you have a great time with. Look at a first date as an experiment where you want to learn more about your date and about yourself. Try to pick a safe place to go that's easy for you; somewhere you are comfortable. Wear something you feel good in and look the best you can. And remember, if you are somewhat anxious, the person you're meeting may be too, so try not to be too judgmental. Even making friends can be a positive thing. Friends can sometimes end up being the love of your life.

57. First Dates

When you meet someone for the first time and you even begin to think about going on a second date there are some cardinal rules to follow.

First, if your date compliments you, accept it! Self-deprecation does not show you have confidence. If they say, "You really look nice tonight" say, "Well, thank you!" not "Oh, I hate the way I look, but I tried." Your inability to accept a compliment might make them rethink the compliment they just gave you!

Second, when you are getting to know someone, try to talk about what is positive. Talking about unpleasant things is never a good way to start a relationship. So keep it light and happy when you want to make a good impression on a first date. (Maybe incorporate this into every date!) You attract what you project. You want happy? Then be that yourself. This doesn't mean you're pretending to be someone you are not; it means positivity outshines negativity every time.

Third, don't talk about your exes—*ever!*—until you have a solid relationship, and then only if they want to know. Talking poorly about any of your past significant others is a waste of everybody's time and/or interest. If you still have a need to talk about any of your past relationships with bitterness or regret, it may mean you're not ready to move on, date, and have a healthy relationship. Men you email, or talk with, will very likely sense this, and it doesn't give them a positive feeling if/when they eventually meet you.

Fourth, it's okay to ask questions; just don't feel that you need to know everything about someone on the first date. Let the conversation flow. Most men don't want to feel they are on a job interview. There are dating coaches who debate about what to ask and what not to ask on a first date. I go with wait until you get to know them better. Things you might not accept on the first date you might accept once you've gotten to know someone. Being too quick to ask and then judging them may mean you could pass up someone whom you might possibly have fallen in love with.

58. When Men Disappear After the First Date

If you start dating and find that you aren't getting asked on second dates ever, or rarely—look to yourself. A thousand men of all ages revealed why they don't ask out women out on second dates. Among the most notable responses: Women who are bossy and want to take charge. Maybe we are nervous or are just trying to show we have confidence. Men get bossed around all the time: previous relationships, their bosses at work...who knows where else. When they first meet you, they simply don't like women who are overly aggressive or want to be in control. Many self-assured, confident, successful women are so used to taking care of everything that they forget this may not be the best approach when first getting to know someone. *This does not mean you have to be whom you are not.* It means taking your time before coming across so assertive and realizing that most men do not like to have someone tell them what to do and when to do it.

59. Be Realistic

If you find there's a lack of interest from those you may be attracted to, try to be objective about yourself and your actual appearance. When looking at profiles, don't focus on the best-looking men on the dating site unless you look a lot like the best-looking female celebrity that pops into your mind. The most handsome men online may look perfect but that doesn't mean they are perfect for you. Give everyone you are even remotely interested in a chance. *And* remember the "tall, dark and handsome" guys in all age groups who have a reasonable and interesting written profile will usually have their inbox filled with female suitors. Why waste your time? There is one exception: if your online profile is outstanding and you have posted appealing photos, that good-looking guy may just end up being attracted to you. Confidence is always a good thing. It won't be the worst thing in the world to not hear back if you do end up emailing him.

60. Safety

I broke every rule in any dating coach's manual and then some on one of my very first dates. The cardinal rule of thumb is *always meet in a safe place.* But intuition plays a big part of who we are as women. I trusted what I felt and so I went to someone's home on a first date. I did this for one reason only—because I wanted to and not because of any pressure he put on me. Of course, we had talked on the phone for many hours and I knew with every instinct I would not be in harm's way, and I wasn't. I knew that. And if my instincts told me once again to do the same, I would. But if you do not trust your instincts and have had bad experiences trusting them, do not do what I did.

It occurs to me as I write this that there exists a certain amount of naïveté in us all. We all make choices and it is *always* better to play it safe and smart. (There were extenuating circumstances, to be explained, surrounding a first date, which is the reason I wrote this book.) Meeting in a public place on a first date or a second or even a third is always the preferred choice. We all have our innate wisdom; whether we recognize or utilize it is up to us. I trusted what I knew to be true and it worked for me...but know your safety and well-being is the top priority when getting to know and meet people you haven't met previously. Also, it doesn't hurt to let a friend or relative know where you are meeting someone and the time frame. And then again, I have recently heard the saying, "Intuition works until it doesn't." So be smart, safe, and aware in online dating.

61. Danger Zone

Let's say you've had a few dates and things look promising. This does not mean you will ignore certain things that may pop up that do not look credible. For instance: does he readily talk about his job, siblings, children? Where he lives? His friends? His interests? You're not looking for specifics immediately, but there are men of all ages who, for whatever reason, cannot be trusted to tell the truth, the whole truth, and nothing but the truth. Recently, I was talking with a friend about her cousin who had supported a man who she had a relationship with for nine years.

For nine years, she chose not to look at the obvious signs and as a result, she had been supporting his drug habit. Do not let this, or anything similar, happen to you. Life is short and you don't want to waste it on men who are deceiving you. If you are handing over your money to someone, you darn well better know where it's going. I also had a close relative whose father-in-law had two families. No one knew this until he was dead and buried. Don't allow yourself to be betrayed like this...the resulting pain and heartbreak are not worth it. If you are awake and alert and use your intuition and have even a modicum of common sense, you will not have this happen to you. Choose wisely who you date. Find men who are trustworthy and who you know will treat and love you as their #1 priority.

Chapter 14—Beyond First Dates

62. In a Committed Relationship

A few important reminders. There appear to be two overriding qualities in relationships. One is respect. When you find someone who respects you, this covers a lot of territory. They will value who you are, what you believe in, and will admire you for what is important to you. The other is safety. You absolutely must feel safe and secure when you are in a relationship. One recent relationship coach in a Ted talk I listened to stated the obvious: your partner will "have your back." That is something we all want; someone who will take care of you and support you no matter what the circumstance may be. If you do not feel safe and secure, you will never feel they "have your back." Unfortunately, it sometimes takes too long to realize that who you thought you knew turns out to be exactly the opposite of who you want in your life. But once you realize this, do not procrastinate the inevitable. You *must move on* if there are any control or domestic violence issues at all.

Dating and becoming involved in a serious relationship can be complicated. Most dating coaches will advise women to go slow and be sure the object of their affection is on the same page. Becoming intimate too soon does not always work the way we want. Getting to know someone takes time...so go slow and get to know who you are dating. And know too, that when you do meet and start a relationship, the "honeymoon" period lasts about two years or more. That is how long it takes to truly get to know a significant other. So don't cut this "getting to know someone" time period short. Those hormones oxytocin, dopamine, and serotonin can overwhelm us and sometimes last longer than we even realize in a new relationship. We can overlook some issues that might not be what we want in a relationship. At least that's what the experts say. It's best not to rush and get in over your head when these feelings take over in a new relationship.

When we approach online dating, the thought of sex and how it will fit into our future relationships is something that cannot be ignored. Sex is part of our human existence and without it, well, where would we be? How we approach this is an individual thing. There are no rights or wrongs, but again, better to be prepared than not. This does not mean to overthink or become obsessively worried about what may or may not happen when we find ourselves attracted to and spending more time with someone. But it does mean that your health and welfare should be a top priority to you.

Mature, stable and honest people will *want* to discuss and be open about their current state of sexual health. Saying, "Oh, I am fine!" should not be acceptable to either party who wants to embark on a sexual relationship with someone. Remember!—whatever measures you take to protect yourself, and others—the only reliable way to know the status of a possible STD is to have testing done. This is an easy, relatively inexpensive thing to do and takes less than a week. After you get the results, you will want to share them with your significant other. This way, there are no surprises down the road if you find yourself with a possible life-altering condition.

When wanting to talk about this with your potential long or even short-term match, you may feel awkward...*just don't move past it without a conversation.* You and your health should be important in any relationship and those who are worthy of your love will feel the same. Sexual intimacy may be and hopefully will be a wonderful part of any relationship. As always, be aware and awake in all aspects of your dating experiences.

63. Why I Wrote This Book

If only I had read similar books like this beforehand, I could have spared myself a lot of pain and heartache. I did not have to go through that experience...and I don't want you to either. I did read and learn more, after the fact, but it was "too little, too late." Be proactive and get a sense of how dating has changed and how people date today. It may be very different from what you experienced when you were single before.

Chapter 15—Heartbreak and Healing

I saw Bart's photos and initially was not attracted to him but liked what he wrote, so I emailed him. He promptly emailed back and thus began our one-sided, very short love affair. He was at his vacation property with family and friends in Arizona and probably just needed to fill up some of his spare time. Hence, Match! It didn't take long to find out we had similar values (or so I thought) and many things in common. I liked him and started projecting into the future.

Red Flag #1: Projecting into the Future

Just because you think you have things in common, or physical attraction or (anything!) doesn't mean a prospective relationship is in the works. Don't project into the future and automatically assume anything. It is a waste of time. Sometimes as women, we try to attach more meaning to things when in reality, it is just that...you have things in common with each other. Until they *show* you who they are by their actions and not just words, don't become invested like I did. Remember, what they do—and not what they say—is all that matters.

While communicating with Bart via phone when he was in Arizona, I had mentioned I was going through a difficult period in my life because of my many significant friends leaving Seattle, including my best friend moving out of the country. I also mentioned that I was having complex hand surgery either in October or January which led him to say, "Oh, have it in October and then you can go to Hawaii with me in January!" I guess that's what prompted me to schedule my surgery in October.

Red Flag #2: What Players Do

Being the inexperienced dater that I was, I believed him! This is what players say when usually they have no intention of taking you anywhere. And certainly not Hawaii. When he buys the tickets and hands them to you, then you will know he intends what he says. Bart undoubtedly forgot this invitation five minutes after he uttered the words. This is a common sign of a player—someone who wants to play with your emotions—all the while just trying to feed their egos. It is common for many men (not all) to do this. Many men are completely unaware that some women actually believe what they say even when it's a flippant remark—though these same men profess that honesty is important to them.

On his trip back home to Seattle from Arizona, Bart called me and we laughed and laughed about a story concerning his dog. We shared the same sense of humor and he was very romantic on the phone and in texts. It didn't hurt that he would tell me how uncommon our conversations were and later how uncommon it was that we were so physically attracted to each other. He was smart, confident, very wealthy, good-looking, and we "got" each other. What was I missing?

Red Flag #3: Jumping to Conclusions

I hadn't even met him but was already on my way to believing he was "The One." Again, it's never good to get involved with your heart before "The One" reveals who he is. Of course, love always involves the heart, but this doesn't mean denying all the red flags you see and sense. I recently saw a series on TV which was a true story involving online dating. The woman time and time again ignored facts she had discovered about "The One" and warnings from her family, and still promptly married him two months after they met...which led to a horrific series of events. Don't be naïve and stay in a situation which will not serve you well. The sooner you wake up and face the truth, the better it will be not only for you but for those who love you and want only the best for you.

Bart arrived in Seattle from Arizona and called me right away from his multimillion-dollar home on the water and wanted me to come over that evening. It had been a particularly difficult day for me after saying goodbye to my spiritual advisor, who was moving out of state. I had just changed my clothes and was ready to take my dog for a walk when he called. I said, "Well, let me think about it." After finding someone in my neighborhood to walk my dog, I called him back and said, "Okay, just know I'm not changing my clothes again. I have yoga pants on and a shirt with half-broken buttons my cat chewed." He didn't seem to have a problem with that and just seemed happy I was coming over.

Red Flag #4: Unworthy

Later down the road, I would reflect and think, was that one of the reasons he disappeared? Because I looked relatively shabby the first time we met, and some of his wealthy neighbors happened to see me? Now I know the answer: *No!* This was not the reason. When we as women get the rug pulled out from underneath us, we try to blame ourselves or think of all the things we did wrong. We picked and trusted someone who was unworthy of our affection. Remember that! *Unworthy of our affection...or time...or love.*

Why did I go to *his* place? For me, it wasn't a safety issue but regardless, *if* he wanted to see me, he should have come to my home or perhaps we should have met in a more neutral location. Maybe the reason was he had driven all day and that was why he didn't offer. Or maybe I was curious to see his place?

Our second date consisted of going out to a small restaurant, where he made comments about how beautiful the server was.

Red Flag #5: Other Women

Men like beautiful women—no surprise here. What should have bothered me was the issue of this being a real first date (our first date being a last-minute get-together), and having him comment on another woman was inappropriate. Later that night, when I was getting ready to drive home at one in the morning in a somewhat unfamiliar part of Seattle, there was nothing said about "text me and let me know you got home safely."

Red Flag #6: Inconsiderate

He didn't text me to make sure I got home because he didn't give a %*#@! Maybe these weren't his thoughts at all, but in hindsight that's how I felt. Did I honestly want a man like that? That alone should have told me: don't waste my time. I want someone who cares about me, don't you? During one date, he left briefly to do something, and I looked over at his phone that had just buzzed...and there was a photo, filling the screen, of a beautiful brunette.

Red Flag #7: Ghosting

He had that very night told me of his last wife's bodily measurements!—and I might add, superior to my own. He went on to tell the story of how he once had ordered a red dress for her from Nordstrom and had it delivered to her office to wear on their opera date that evening. Did I really need to know this? Plus, who leaves his phone out on a date when still connected to Match? I wish I had just gotten up, left, and said, "Maybe you want to get back to your dating site? Bye." And remember, if anyone is more concerned with their phone and even has their phone out when they're getting to know you and are with you—what does this tell you?

So...we had a few more dates, sitting on his roof top listening to music complete with an outdoor fireplace, overlooking our beautiful city of Seattle and the stars and the full moon.

Our very last date ended with me watching him walking away with his dog. I knew something wasn't right, and it wasn't. Welcome to the new world of ghosting...which led to my broken heart.

If I can prevent five women—no, even one woman!—from going through what I did, it will have been worth every minute of my time spent writing this book. Many of us have experienced heartache and know it is one of the most painful things we humans can endure. I was ready emotionally and did want to find love and believed it could happen. It had been almost four years since my husband's death, thirty-seven years of marriage and forty years since dating. I found out quickly that I did not intellectually or emotionally prepare myself for things that can happen and what to be aware of when starting this adventure.

Ghosting...what is that? I had no clue until it was too late. Read whatever you can to learn as much as you can before jumping in with your heart. As stated previously, there are now many books and free online videos by numerous dating coaches. Take advantage of these. If you have read what I've written, you have learned maybe a little to get you started on the right track. I was naïve, trusting, open-hearted, and had not a clue about how dating had changed. I hadn't kissed someone other than my husband in forty years.

Why did I even believe I could get entangled with someone so experienced without having more information? Even though our intimacy was consensual, I did feel somewhat taken advantage of because he knew I was a somewhat recent widow and that dating was a new experience for me. This is why learning about and being assured of how to approach "new" dating scenarios are better learned *before* not *after* doing anything you may regret later.

Bart talked mostly about himself and his family and I don't think he ever asked about mine or who I was or what was important to me. I think this was one reason I got a broken heart. I did not understand that this is how *some* men will treat you—*if* you let them. During the next six months, and I am totally embarrassed to say this, I cried more than all of my years on the planet combined. I never knew my body could hold that much water.

Looking back at this painful time, I suspect it was a combination of what was a perfect storm—so many of my good friends and my spiritual advisor leaving this area, and the death of my oldest sister, all happening close to our meeting. He was a big part of my grief, but not the entire reason. I would have been able to accept him saying, "Mary, it just won't work for us. I am unable to see you anymore." That would have been understandable...but when this ghosting occurs and you have never experienced it before, you wonder: "Did he die?" (serious here.) "Did his previous girlfriend, ex-wife, or new love appear on the scene?" "Does he have a health issue he doesn't want me to have to deal with?"

When a person cuts off all communication due to unstable personalities, harassment, or stalking and/or unwanted advances, then that is totally acceptable. This is not classified as "ghosting" but an attempt at self-preservation, and is a necessary thing to do. The ghosting that is so prevalent today occurs when there is a legitimate connection between two adults who both seem to have an agreement that there is a least a modicum of respect and mutual attraction for each other...until one drops out of sight.

A coward will walk away and neglect to give a simple reason for their decision to end things.

The main reason is that they are thinking only of themselves and trying to make it easier for them. They are probably "conflict avoiders." Easier for them to leave with the excuse that they didn't want to have any sort of conflict, or not wanting to "hurt your feelings."

Bart was supposedly a mature man, not a twenty or thirty-year-old who would not possess the ability to decide reasonably how to end a short affair. This does not take effort; it only takes kindness, which, I felt, he did not exhibit. Do not ever believe that ghosting is an acceptable form of behavior. All kinds of men and women do this in online dating, but that doesn't make it okay. Ghosting is not walking away after one date or even two or three. It happens when some form of intimacy has occurred.

We are in a new era. Because it has become easy to say whatever we want online in any form, it has now morphed into it being okay in person: to say or do anything that makes you feel okay without regard for the other person. And there remains karma...but we shouldn't be considerate and kind because we're afraid of payback later on down the road. We treat others the way we want to be treated because that is what is important and reveals the kind of person we are or want to be. When we respect others with decency and kindness, we will attract others who value what we do and those who are similar to who we are.

There are dating coaches who seem to think, "Oh, it's okay, men just change their minds." Yes, both men and women, can and do change their minds, but saying what you want to get what you want and then disappearing may not be a kind way to end any type of relationship— short or long. Some women and men too, may wonder what *is* the best way to untangle? There is no set rule to this, but the overriding concern is to remember sometimes the only way out is through. Tell them face to face if at all possible and keep it short and simple: "I'm sorry, but it just won't work for us." No need to list the ninety-nine reasons why you believe this to be true.

If you don't want someone whom you were attracted to and had intimate moments with to disappear into the ether without a word, why would you think they'd want you to do the same? It all comes down to respect for other people. Yes, it can be very difficult to end a relation-ship, but all it takes is a little bravery and courage to do what is right. You, and they, will feel things ended in the best possible way and there will be no guilt or misgivings when moving on.

Another note on ghosting: if you are very self-assured or a confident veteran of dating, this phenomenon may not affect you the way it did me. If you can move on quickly and have no regrets when men, whom you have feelings for, drop you without a word, I say good for you! This is how you want to react. They are not worth your time or even thoughts if they can't give you the respect you deserve.

At the very time I was writing this paragraph—and I am not making this up—the Ghost's profile once again popped up on Match. It was also his birthday. He had sent me a picture of his grandson and him, complete with his birthday cake, exactly one year ago to the day! Here he was, on his birthday a year later, still scrolling, looking for that elusive someone to fulfill his needs. I assumed the probability was high that he was unable to sustain a relationship after his ghosting me. I decided to email him twice, right then, and did some groveling, to finally confirm that he was not the significant other I was looking for or desiring. Confirmed! He failed the test. I now was free because I knew that he was not good enough for me.

The primary reason for retelling my experience with you is for you to be aware of men who care more about themselves than about you. Don't spend one minute thinking about someone who doesn't have the emotional capability to treat you with kindness and at least a token amount of caring. Was he a bad person? No, he wasn't. He had many good qualities, was very accomplished, had a nice family, friends, and cared for others I'm sure—but he appeared to me, in our very short time together, as just a player who wanted the immediate, perfect soulmate, not understanding that love of any substance usually takes time. Was he, as many, many men and women are, unable to accept others' imperfections, even though they themselves have imperfections, including physical limitations and other issues of their own? Sooner or later they realize that what they are looking for simply doesn't exist in our human existence...there is no perfection.

From this very painful time, a few positive things happened that for me were life-altering. One, I now knew that I could love someone again and two, sometimes the painful and difficult times we have will open new doors and force us to look at ourselves and our world in a different way. I still believed that something good would happen.

Coming Around Again

I know nothing stays the same,

but if you're willing to play the game

It's coming around again.

So don't mind if I fall apart

There's more room in a broken heart.

And I believe in Love...I believe in Love

I do believe in Love, I do believe in Love...

And it's coming around again....

—a somewhat dated song by Carly Simon but still true

....As fate would have it, the pilot from the beginning of this book and I are now dating and in a committed relationship. To me, he is the kindest, most passionate, most loving, caring, handsome, smart, genuine guy who makes me happy and makes me laugh. And yes!—we have traveled to Hawaii. I don't know what the future holds but I know what we have right now is love. And that is what the Universe will bring to you *if you believe* it.

FINAL THOUGHTS

Believe Online Dating is Worth It

...it may take a change of attitude to understand and accept this because many of your friends and even you may question why you would even consider it. Online dating does work and statistics prove it. Just because some of your married or even single friends think it's a scary, bad, silly idea doesn't mean it is. This book can help you find a significant other who treats you as you deserve to be treated and loved. It was written to give you a head start as you enter this occasionally confusing game of dating. But it's like anything else; practice makes perfect. The more you face your fears and conquer your anxiety, the faster it will turn into a positive experience.

Believe in Yourself

...have confidence in who you are and let it show. This is the most important thing you simply have to understand. You are good enough. You *can* find someone even if you don't have the perfect body weight or shape, or run half–marathons. You *can* find someone as long as you are accepting, believe in love, and don't expect perfection in a significant other.

Be Proactive

...you can believe in yourself all you want—but that alone won't get you where you want to be. You simply have to put fear aside and do what it takes to meet your match. Online dating, even with its many drawbacks, is still a good way to meet men. If it seems overwhelming, *take at least one small step*. Even glancing at the various dating sites is something you can do...and inevitably you will realize it is easier than you thought.

Understand That You Can Recover from Past Wounds

...if you haven't recovered from a past relationship and aren't totally over it, wait until you are. When you are wounded, you will attract others who are wounded and stuck too. Subconsciously, you will view current relationships through the lens of your past painful one. Seek help. A counselor/therapist can help you arrive at your full potential and help you realize what you want in your life. It may take work and counseling to figure out what you need to do to overcome issues such as unhappiness or lack of self-esteem. People want to be with someone who is a happy, stable person and who is ready to be part of a healthy relationship. Don't look for someone to make you happy and don't think someone else can "cure" you of deep-seated problems. Work on overcoming them *before* trying to meet anyone. Like attracts like. When you can achieve happiness within yourself and like yourself, you will attract someone who also likes who they are.

Figure Out What You Want in Your Life

...don't believe it's too late, no matter what your age. Maybe the process is a little different than you could have ever imagined. But life is about change and the happiest people are those who can adapt. Forget your fears and look at online dating like a new adventure even though you may have tried it previously.

Come Up with the Best Profile You Possibly Can, and Get Help if You Need It

...pick a catchy username. Take your time in selecting your photos. Use the very best photos you have of yourself. Don't rush and go online without a decently written profile. It needs to be properly written and grammatically correct with no misspellings. Use coherent paragraphs about who you are and what you want. Be positive!

Read About Online Dating, and Watch Videos Too

...in addition to this book, you can find resources that are cheap, easy, and fast to read or view that can give you an idea of what you may experience. There are lots of videos and good dating advice on the internet for free and there are many dating coaches who are happy to tell you what to do and what not to do for a fee. Seek and you shall find. Dating has changed. There is absolutely nothing wrong with online dating *if* you use your intuition and intelligence in choosing your dates, and are prepared.

Get a Life

...make yours interesting. Keep doing things with your friends, do things you've never done before, go places you've never been. Get over being afraid of everything. When you have achieved this, you will entice that person you like to be interested in you, and it will make them want to be part of your exciting life. I had always wanted to sail and decided to take a week-long sailing cruise on the Hopscotch in the San Juan Islands here in Washington State. It was an incredible trip and the best part was my now significant other flew up to have lunch with me while we were docked at Friday Harbor, a beautiful seaside resort town. Keep your life fascinating and you will find others who are fascinated by you. Wherever you live, you can and will want to be part of a group or organization, including volunteering in your community. Even if you work full time, try your hardest to get out in your community even if it's just hanging out in your local Starbucks. An acquaintance of mine met an incredibly nice guy at our local Starbucks. They traveled all over the world and were wonderful together.

First Dates

...try to look at a first date as a chance to meet someone you don't know but who might possibly become a good friend, even if they don't turn out to be the love of your life. But sometimes friends can eventually end up being your soulmate. I am proof positive of that.

When I first met my now significant other, there was no instant chemistry. I did like him and thought we could be friends, but it was only on our third date, over a year later, that sparks flew and we have been together ever since that day. I was proactive—asked him to a fundraiser I had an extra ticket to (our third date), I was motivated—emailed him occasionally since our first date, mostly because I liked his sense of humor and finally, I was patient—it was about timing. We were each going through things with other people and then destiny occurred... we finally did have a third date and something magical happened. No one will ever convince me that what happened between us wasn't my belief—that love can happen when you believe it will.

Red Flags
...you simply must know what you want! Do you want to be married or remarried? Then don't spend time with someone who says, "I will never marry or remarry." Is one of your life's goals travel? Then don't try to have a relationship with someone who is a homebody and not interested in travel. These are simple examples. Just don't get caught up investing your time with someone who represents what you don't want in your life. And it's important to notice these red flags *sooner rather than later*. There is more than one person who will give you what you need in your life; don't waste your time taking the road that leads you to the wrong place.

Rejection
...going on dates and being rejected and finding out there is no chemistry whatsoever is difficult. Instead of going with the expectation of "this will be a perfect date and I know he is 'The One,'" look at it as an opportunity to simply have a good time. When you first meet someone with a relaxed feeling, you will reveal who you truly are. And remember, the

more dates you have, the easier it becomes and the less anxious you will be. If it doesn't work, brush yourself off and don't give up. I know someone who had picked an outfit that she wore to every first date. She looked good in it and felt comfortable, so why not!? Think of the time and expense this saves! There is absolutely no reason to spend a fortune on new clothes. Invest in one or two outfits you look good in and wear the same thing on all first dates.

Timing

...remember the old saying, "Rome wasn't built in a day"? Well, finding your ideal someone won't take as long as building Rome, but it may not happen overnight. Try to stay positive, believe in the process, and be proactive. If you see someone who interests you, don't be shy. Email them! Men like to be approached first. The old adages no longer apply in this new way of meeting prospective significant others. Many of us remember the days when asking men first to do anything was definitely unacceptable. But times have changed. If you write a decent profile and post your best photos, you will get some responses. Online dating takes effort. The most important thing to remember is never, ever give up.

Intuition

...always follow your intuition. When you know something isn't working, pay attention. Either change what you are doing or move on. Don't hesitate and make things worse. If something doesn't feel right, it more than likely isn't. And if friends or relatives show some concern, listen to them. They're looking out for your welfare, and may be more observant about what is happening. Sometimes when we involve our hearts, it's difficult to be objective and we miss certain signs that we normally wouldn't. Most of us have good intuition; don't ever forget that. But however good our intuition is, we must pay attention to how a possible match treats us and if we feel completely safe around them. Worthy and honest men will be open, want you to meet friends and family, and will not be afraid to tell you how they spend their time when not with you. Your safety and future safety depend on your being awake and aware.

Best wishes on your journey and don't forget...*believe in love!*

EPILOGUE

As I was finishing this book, I realized my true intent is not just about helping others find a significant other or the love of their lives. It's also about believing in who we are and realizing that what we want in our lives can become a reality no matter what it is we desire. When we have the courage to get outside of our comfort zones and truly *believe*, we can find what will bring us true happiness.

During the time I was trying to get this book published, I would meet or listen to other authors and be amazed at what they were writing. Coming from the genre of non-fiction, many had advanced degrees and were doctors, psychologists, attorneys, or celebrities, along with others from all different walks of life and occupations. No matter who they were, or from what background, they all wrote about something that was meaningful to them. As I would hear these authors speak and see their dedication, I realized that they had two major things in common—they were passionate about what they knew or had experienced and they wanted to help other people by sharing what they had learned.

I came to the realization that this book can be used in every area of your life; when you face rejection, when you need resilience, when you need to practice forgiveness—these things I hope you have learned about dating you can use every day. Love is the most important part of who we are as humans. Don't ever give up the search for love *and* the understanding that you can best serve the world by believing in yourself.

ACKNOWLEDGMENTS

First, I would like to thank my friend and counselor, Kari O'Neill, who encouraged me but was truthful in her first remark that publishing a book is not what it used to be. Enter the digital age! As the very first person to read my finished manuscript, it was valuable to me that she thought women trying online dating could benefit and find support from reading it.

My gratitude is also extended to my high school English teacher, Mrs. Pate. She gave me the love of words and an understanding of how to write a sentence...correctly.

I want to thank my many friends and acquaintances whose input ended up in the book. Their experiences with online dating and the stories they related added to what I wanted to write in my quest to help women overcome their fears as they search for love. And thanks to Bob Sherwin, a screenwriter, who gave the book an optimistic review.

Thanks to Chin-Sun Lee who edited my book and made it better. I appreciated her suggestions and knowledgeable input. Many thanks to Natalie Post of postproductions.com for her photography skills and to Kevin Smith, the graphic artist who designed my book cover and responded with patience to my many requests. Also, thanks to Dr. Sarah Brown who encouraged me and answered technical questions relating to the hard part: marketing and publication. Much gratitude and appreciation to Meili Cady for her great ideas and promoting my book in all media venues.

Last, but not least is Ken, my loving partner who supported and encouraged me throughout the writing and publishing of this book. His 'tech' help and 'being there' at all times has meant the world to me.

ABOUT THE AUTHOR

Mary Hyatt Doerrer grew up in a small town in southern Indiana, but has lived most of her life in Seattle. She loves the people, the trees but maybe not so much the rain. She has been a church moderator, dental hygienist, protestor, crisis clinic volunteer, ski shop employee, parks commissioner, and now is happily staying home with her significant other. Her two adult children live close by. This is her first book.